Mindful Masculinity: An Anger Management Workbook for Men

Empowering Men to Navigate Anger with Wisdom and Compassion

Alex Carter

Table of Contents

INTRODUCTION

"Mindful Masculinity: An Anger Management Workbook for Men - Empowering Men to Navigate Anger with Wisdom and Compassion" is a transformative e-book designed to address the complex and often overlooked issue of anger management in men. Authored with a deep understanding of the unique challenges men face in today's society, this comprehensive workbook blends the principles of mindfulness with the exploration of masculinity, providing a roadmap for individuals to cultivate emotional intelligence and resilience.

In a world that frequently imposes societal expectations on men to suppress emotions, particularly anger, this e- book aims to break the silence and stigma surrounding male emotions. It invites readers on a journey of self- discovery, encouraging them to embrace a mindful approach to understanding and managing anger. Drawing upon ancient mindfulness practices and contemporary therapeutic techniques, the workbook offers practical exercises, reflective prompts, and actionable strategies to help men channel their anger in healthy and constructive ways.

The narrative unfolds with sensitivity, recognizing the diversity of experiences and acknowledging the impact of societal norms on men's emotional well-being. Mindful masculinity goes beyond traditional anger management approaches by delving into the roots of anger, exploring its triggers, and fostering a compassionate understanding of one's own emotions. The workbook also addresses the interconnectedness of anger with other aspects of masculinity, relationships, and mental health, fostering a holistic approach to personal growth.

As an empowering resource, this e-book equips men with the tools to navigate their emotions with wisdom and compassion. It advocates for a masculinity that embraces vulnerability and self-awareness, challenging stereotypes and fostering a healthier, more resilient approach to anger management. Mindful masculinity is a beacon for men seeking to cultivate emotional well-being, enabling positive transformations in their personal and interpersonal lives.

CHAPTER I

Unpacking Anger

Defining Anger

Anger, a fundamental human emotion, is a complex and multifaceted phenomenon that has intrigued psychologists, philosophers, and scientists for centuries. Defined as a strong feeling of displeasure and belligerence, anger encompasses a broad spectrum of emotional experiences, ranging from mild irritation to intense rage. To truly understand anger, one must delve into its origins, physiological manifestations, psychological underpinnings, and the societal implications it carries.

At its core, anger is a natural response to perceived threats or injustices. Rooted in the primitive fight-or-flight response, anger emerges when an individual feels their well-being or values are jeopardized. The physiological cascade accompanying anger involves the release of stress hormones, heightened heart rate, and increased blood pressure. This visceral reaction prepares the body for action, a mechanism deeply ingrained in our evolutionary history as a means of survival.

However, the expression of anger is not solely governed by instinct; it is also intricately intertwined with cognitive processes and individual differences. Cultural, social, and personal factors play pivotal roles in shaping how anger is perceived and managed. Some societies encourage the open expression of anger as a form of assertiveness, while others emphasize restraint and emotional control. Consequently, the subjective experience of anger varies widely among individuals, reflecting the intricate interplay between nature and nurture.

Psychologically, anger has been dissected through various theoretical lenses. Psychodynamic perspectives posit that anger is often a manifestation of repressed emotions and unresolved conflicts from childhood. Cognitive models, on the other hand, highlight the role of distorted thinking patterns and irrational beliefs in fueling anger. Understanding these underlying mechanisms is crucial for developing effective therapeutic interventions for anger management.

Moreover, anger is not a monolithic emotion; it exists on a continuum with related emotions such as frustration, resentment, and hostility. Distinguishing between healthy and destructive expressions of anger is imperative for fostering emotional well-being. While healthy anger can prompt assertiveness and drive positive change, unbridled rage may lead to aggression, violence, and long-term psychological harm.

In interpersonal relationships, anger can be both a catalyst for conflict and a tool for resolution. The ability to express anger assertively, without resorting to aggression, is essential for maintaining healthy communication. Conversely, unresolved anger can erode relationships, creating a cycle of resentment and hatred. Effective anger management strategies, including active listening, empathy, and conflict resolution skills, are indispensable for fostering constructive dialogue and maintaining harmonious connections.

Society, too, is profoundly impacted by the collective expression of anger. Social movements driven by a shared sense of injustice exemplify the constructive potential of collective rage, channeling it into calls for systemic change. However, when societal anger is not directed productively, it can lead to polarization, violence, and social unrest. Understanding the dynamics of collective anger is crucial for policymakers, activists, and citizens alike, as it shapes the course of social and political landscapes.

In conclusion, the multifaceted nature of anger necessitates a comprehensive exploration that spans biological, psychological, and sociocultural dimensions. Acknowledging anger as a universal human experience allows for a nuanced understanding of its role in shaping individual and collective behavior. By unraveling the complexities of rage, we pave the way for effective anger management, healthier relationships, and a more empathetic society.

Identifying Triggers

The human psyche is a complex tapestry of emotions, and at the heart of this intricate weave lies the concept of triggers. In the psychological sense, triggers evoke intense emotional reactions, often tied to past experiences or deeply ingrained beliefs. Identifying these triggers is a critical step in understanding our emotional responses and navigating the labyrinth of our inner world. By unraveling the layers of triggers, we gain insight into the roots of our emotional reactions, empowering us to cultivate greater self-awareness, emotional intelligence, and resilience.

Triggers can be as varied as the human experience, spanning a spectrum of internal and external stimuli. Internally, triggers may be rooted in unresolved traumas, unmet needs, or core beliefs shaped by early life experiences. External triggers, on the other hand, can manifest as specific situations, words, or behaviors exhibited by others. These triggers can stir emotions, sometimes leading to reactions that seem disproportionate to the apparent cause. The intricate dance between internal and external triggers shapes the landscape of our emotional responses, creating a mosaic unique to each individual.

Unraveling the web of triggers begins with introspection and a willingness to explore the recesses of our minds. Journaling, mindfulness practices, and therapy are invaluable tools for peeling back the layers of our emotional responses. Through these processes, we can identify recurrent patterns and themes, shedding light on the origins of our triggers. For some, a seemingly innocuous comment may tap into a deep-seated fear of rejection, while for others, a specific tone of voice might transport them back to a traumatic past. Understanding these connections is pivotal in dismantling the power of triggers and reclaiming emotional agency.

Furthermore, the role of cognitive processes in trigger identification must be considered. Our thoughts and interpretations play a crucial role in shaping emotional responses. Cognitive distortions, such as black-and-white thinking or catastrophizing, can amplify the impact of triggers, intensifying emotional reactions. By honing mental awareness, individuals can learn to challenge and reframe distorted thoughts, mitigating the influence of triggers on their emotional well-being.

Social interactions, a rich source of external triggers, also contribute significantly to the tapestry of our emotional responses. Miscommunications, unmet expectations, and perceived slights in relationships can act as powerful triggers, eliciting emotional reactions that may seem disproportionate in the moment. Developing practical communication skills, empathy, and conflict-resolution strategies is essential for navigating interpersonal triggers. Additionally, fostering a culture of emotional openness and vulnerability within relationships can create a supportive environment for individuals to explore and address their triggers collaboratively.

The workplace, another arena with potential triggers, demands a nuanced understanding of individual and collective emotional landscapes. Stressors such as tight deadlines, high expectations, or interpersonal conflicts can act as triggers, impacting job satisfaction and overall well-being. Organizations that prioritize emotional intelligence, provide resources for stress management, and cultivate a positive work environment can mitigate workplace triggers and foster employee resilience.

Moreover, the impact of societal and cultural factors on trigger identification must be addressed. Cultural norms, societal expectations, and systemic inequalities shape how individuals perceive and respond to triggers. Acknowledging and challenging societal norms that contribute to the marginalization of certain groups is crucial for creating a more inclusive and equitable society. The intersectionality of triggers, where individual, interpersonal, and societal factors converge, highlights the need for a holistic approach to trigger identification and management.

In conclusion, identifying triggers is a dynamic and ongoing process requiring self-reflection, cognitive awareness, and understanding of the intricate interplay between internal and external stimuli. By unraveling the layers of triggers, individuals can gain profound insights into the roots of their emotional responses, paving the way for personal growth and emotional resilience. As we navigate the complex tapestry of triggers, individually and collectively, we embark on a journey toward greater self-awareness, compassion, and a more nuanced understanding of the intricate dance between our inner world and the external environment.

Recognizing the Physical and Emotional Manifestations of Anger

Anger, a primal and pervasive human emotion, manifests in a dynamic interplay of physical and emotional responses ranging from subtle irritation to explosive rage. Recognizing anger's multifaceted manifestations is crucial for understanding its impact on individuals and society. This section delves into the intricate tapestry of anger, exploring the physiological and psychological dimensions that give rise to its diverse expressions.

Physiologically, anger sets a cascade of bodily responses finely tuned by evolution to prepare an individual for action. When faced with a perceived threat or injustice, the body releases stress hormones, such as adrenaline and cortisol, triggering the "fight or flight" response. This results in an increased heart rate, elevated blood pressure, and heightened alertness—an adaptive mechanism to enhance physical performance. While evolutionarily advantageous, these physiological changes underscore the visceral nature of anger and its roots in the survival instincts of our ancestors.

The physical manifestations of anger extend beyond the immediate fight-or-flight response. Chronic anger has been linked to a myriad of health issues, including cardiovascular problems, compromised immune function, and increased susceptibility to mental health disorders. The prolonged activation of the stress response system, if left unchecked, can contribute to various medical conditions, highlighting the intricate connection between emotional well-being and physical health.

Beyond the physiological realm, anger profoundly influences cognitive processes and emotional regulation. The mental manifestations of anger often involve distorted thinking patterns, where individuals may engage in black-and-white thinking, magnification of perceived slights, or the attribution of hostile intent to others. These cognitive distortions fuel the intensity of anger, contributing to a cycle of negative thoughts and emotions.

Emotionally, anger encompasses a broad spectrum of experiences, ranging from mild frustration to overwhelming fury. Understanding this range requires exploring how anger is expressed and the underlying emotions that may coexist with it. Beneath the surface of anger, one may find fear, hurt, or feelings of powerlessness—emotional layers that, when unearthed, provide a more comprehensive understanding of the individual's internal landscape.

The expression of anger is not uniform across individuals or cultures, and societal norms play a significant role in shaping how anger is perceived and managed. Some cultures may encourage the open expression of anger as a sign of assertiveness, while others may prioritize emotional restraint and self-control. The societal expectations surrounding gender, too, contribute to the diversity in anger expression, with research suggesting that societal norms may influence how men and women are socialized to express or suppress anger.

In interpersonal relationships, recognizing the emotional manifestations of anger is pivotal for effective communication and conflict resolution. Unexpressed or mismanaged anger can give rise to passive-aggressive behaviors, simmering resentment, and a communication breakdown. Conversely, when done assertively and constructively, the open expression of anger can catalyze addressing underlying issues and fostering healthier relationships.

Moreover, the emotional manifestations of anger extend to the broader societal context. Social movements driven by collective anger highlight the transformative potential of shared outrage in challenging systemic injustices. However, the mismanagement of societal anger can lead to polarization, violence, and social unrest. Recognizing and channeling collective anger toward positive change requires a nuanced understanding of the underlying issues and a commitment to constructive dialogue and social reform.

The intertwining of physical and emotional manifestations of anger underscores the importance of holistic approaches to anger management. Cognitive-behavioral therapy, mindfulness practices, and emotion regulation techniques are among the therapeutic interventions designed to address both the cognitive and emotional aspects of anger. These approaches aim to equip individuals with the tools to identify and challenge distorted thoughts, regulate intense emotions, and develop healthier coping mechanisms.

In conclusion, recognizing anger's physical and emotional manifestations unveils a complex tapestry that weaves together physiological responses, cognitive processes, and emotional experiences. The interplay between these dimensions shapes the diverse ways anger is expressed and underscores its profound impact on individual well-being and societal dynamics. By fostering a nuanced understanding of anger, we pave the way for effective anger management, healthier relationships, and a more empathetic and socially conscious society.

CHAPTER II

The Societal Context

Cultural Expectations of Masculinity

Masculinity, a social construct intricately woven into the fabric of diverse cultures, is a dynamic and evolving concept that shapes the identities and behaviors of men across the globe. Cultural expectations of masculinity dictate norms, values, and behaviors deemed acceptable within a given society, often influencing individual self-perception and interpersonal dynamics. This section explores the complicated terrain of cultural norms around masculinity, including its roots, expressions, and significant effects on individuals and society.

Historical, sociological, and economic settings play a significant role in shaping cultural standards of masculinity. Historically, characteristics like power, stoicism, assertiveness, and the capacity to provide for and defend others have been linked to masculinity. These beliefs are frequently a result of men's historical responsibilities as hunters, fighters, and breadwinners. Even if these roles have changed, cultural standards and how masculinity is viewed and demonstrated are still shaped by the lingering effects of earlier expectations.

Rigid gender roles established by many societies demonstrate the performative character of masculinity. It's common for men to be expected to exhibit features that are considered "masculine" and to shun those linked to femininity. In addition to restricting the spectrum of appropriate masculinity expressions, this binary framework feeds negative stereotypes and upholds gender inequity. Genuine self-expression is severely hampered for men who stray from these socially acceptable standards because they risk humiliation, mockery, or even social exclusion.

The influence of societal norms around masculinity is felt in many areas of men's lives, such as relationships, mental health, and professional goals. The suppression of emotions, especially vulnerability and melancholy, can be attributed to the pressure to live up to society's expectations of being a man. Men may internalize that they should be strict and unwavering, making it more challenging to ask for emotional help and find healthy ways to manage stress. The repression of emotions has been connected, in turn, to increased incidence of mental health problems such as substance misuse and depression.

Cultural norms surrounding masculinity influence interpersonal relationships between men and women and among the male population. Toxic masculinity is typified by aggression, dominance, and the rejection of characteristics deemed "weak" or "feminine." It is exacerbated by pressure to fit in with prevailing ideas of masculinity. Toxic masculinity not only perpetuates negative power dynamics but also obstructs real connection and emotional intimacy in relationships.

Furthermore, the professions men choose to pursue and the leadership philosophies they adopt indicate how cultural expectations of masculinity impact career goals. Societal conventions frequently influence men to pursue occupations that conform to stereotypical ideas of being a man, such as engineering, finance, or physically demanding jobs. Men being expected to be the primary providers for their families can also lead to workaholism, stress, and a reluctance to explore less profitable but more meaningful occupations.

Because different cultures may emphasize various components of masculinity, the impact of cultural expectations of masculinity varies between societies. For instance, whereas some cultures value individual success and assertiveness, others place a higher value on collectivism and emphasize community and family. The experiences of males in various cultural contexts are made even more complex by the interconnectedness of masculinity with other cultural characteristics like race, ethnicity, and financial class.

The movement to rethink and question societal norms surrounding masculinity has gathered steam in the last several years. The goal of movements supporting gender equality and the demolition of damaging stereotypes is to develop a broader, more compassionate definition of masculinity. Well-known people in the media, academia, and activism are questioning the status quo and pushing males to be open to showing vulnerability, expressing the whole gamut of emotions, and building respectful, communication-based, healthy relationships.

Redefining cultural expectations of masculinity is primarily dependent on education. Teachers may help future generations develop a more complex sense of masculinity by advocating gender-sensitive courses that question stereotypes and promote critical thinking. Opening up dialogue on gender roles and expectations contributes to the eradication of harmful stereotypes and the advancement of an inclusive and accepting society.

In summary, cultural norms around masculinity are a potent force influencing men's identities, conduct, and general well-being in various societies. Rooted in historical and sociological contexts, the performative aspect of masculinity adds to a complicated web of expectations that impact relationships, job aspirations, and mental health. A vital first step in establishing genuine self-expression, advancing gender equality, and building a more accepting and compassionate society is realizing and opposing these expectations. We must accept diversity, dispel negative stereotypes, and free people to develop their identities free from the shackles of inflexible cultural norms as we negotiate the maze of masculinity.

The Stigma Surrounding Men and Emotional Expression

In the intricate tapestry of human experience, emotions are the threads weaving the fabric of our lives. Yet, within the realm of emotional expression, a pervasive and often unspoken stigma surrounds men. The culturally imposed notions of masculinity place restrictions on the range of emotions that men are permitted to experience. This section explores the many facets of the stigma associated with men expressing their emotions, including its historical roots, effects on relationships, mental health, and cultural dynamics, as well as the current initiatives to challenge these deeply embedded conventions.

Traditional gender roles and societal expectations are the source of the stigma that surrounds men and emotional expressiveness. Men have traditionally been conditioned to represent virtues like emotional stoicism, strength, and resilience. These expectations, which are ingrained in cultural narratives, stigmatize vulnerability, sensitivity, and the expression of so-called "soft" emotions while prescribing a limited spectrum of acceptable emotional manifestations for men. Men are prevented from expressing their emotions honestly by the strong barrier created by the media, socialization, and interpersonal dynamics that promote these gender standards.

Men suppressing their emotions is one of the main effects of this stigma. Because men are expected to be independent and emotionally challenged by society, they tend to internalize their problems and hide their weaknesses. Emotional suppression brought on by the pressure to fit in with these norms can eventually lead to a variety of mental health problems, such as anxiety, sadness, and an increased risk of substance dependence.

The cycle of silent suffering is prolonged when people are reluctant to ask for assistance or talk about emotional problems.

Toxic masculinity, which is defined by strict gender roles and the rejection of feelings thought to be incompatible with traditional masculinity, is encouraged in the context of interpersonal relationships by the stigma attached to men and emotional expression. In addition to impeding sincere emotional closeness and connection, toxic masculinity also supports aggressiveness, power disparities, and the maintenance of negative stereotypes. Because they are expected to value strength over vulnerability, men who follow these norms may find it challenging to negotiate sexual relationships, friendships, and familial ties. This makes it difficult for them to connect with others genuinely.

Moreover, the workplace becomes a theater of complex conflicts where the stigma associated with men and emotional expressiveness is expressed. While qualities like emotional intelligence, empathy, and teamwork may be discounted, assertiveness, dominance, and unwavering confidence are frequently valued in traditional conceptions of masculinity. Men who don't live up to these standards could suffer from biased reviews and restricted career advancement, among other adverse effects. In the workplace, there might be pressure to uphold stereotypically masculine habits, which can lead to increased stress, burnout, and a generalized feeling of loneliness.

Another critical factor in the stigma that surrounds men and emotional expression is societal dynamics. Men's experiences are made more complex by the interaction of gender with other sociocultural elements, including race, ethnicity, and socioeconomic class. Men of color, for example, could face additional prejudices that converge with conventional notions of masculinity and impact how they negotiate emotional expression in their communities and society at large.

In recent years, there has been a growing movement to combat the stigma associated with men expressing their emotions. Movements for mental health, cultural changes, and advocacy are helping to create a more inclusive definition of masculinity. Well-known people from a variety of industries are speaking up about their mental health issues, questioning social standards, and urging men to see vulnerability as a strength rather than a weakness. These discussions aim to break down the stigma and provide guys with a safe area to express themselves without worrying about criticism or backlash.

Education is shown to be a potent instrument for changing cultural perceptions of men and emotional expressiveness. One way to help break down the barriers around male emotional expression is to introduce broad curricula curricula that question old gender conventions, promote empathy, and foster emotional intelligence. Establishing environments where students feel inspired to explore and express their feelings without feeling pressured to adhere to gender-specific norms is something that educational institutions can do a great deal to support.

Mental health practitioners are realizing how critical it is to address men's particular difficulties with expressing their emotions in therapy settings. Men's emotional well-being requires culturally aware techniques that affirm a range of emotional experiences, dispel negative preconceptions, and promote candid communication. Group therapy, mentorship programs, and community-based projects offer forums for men to confront societal standards, share their stories, and work together to eliminate the stigma of expressing their emotions.

In addition, how men are portrayed in the media greatly influences how society views males and how they express their emotions. By performing a varied array of masculine people who genuinely manage their emotions, the media has the power to contest stereotypes and foster a more sophisticated comprehension of masculinity. The propagation of virtuous role models who place a high value on emotional intelligence, empathy, and vulnerability can significantly influence public opinion and undermine deeply embedded stigmas.

In conclusion, a strongly ingrained part of cultural standards and expectations is the stigma associated with men expressing their emotions. This stigma negatively impacts men's relationships, career aspirations, and mental health. It takes a multifaceted approach incorporating education, media representation, and cultural shifts to recognize and demolish these deeply rooted conventions. We help men navigate the complex emotional landscape, releasing themselves from the constraints of social expectations and embracing the full range of their humanity by creating surroundings that value authenticity and vulnerability.

Breaking Down Stereotypes

Stereotypes, those ingrained and often oversimplified beliefs about a particular group of people, persist as formidable barriers to genuine understanding and inclusivity. This section explores the complexities surrounding stereotypes, investigating their origins, perpetuation, and the profound impacts they wield on individuals and society. By examining the different shapes stereotypes take, their effects on oppressed groups, and our shared need to destroy them, we hope to shed light on how to promote a more just and compassionate society.

Stereotypes are firmly ingrained in the human mind and result from cultural prejudices and cognitive shortcuts. They frequently appear as mental heuristics that help people sort and make sense of the enormous amount of information they come across daily. However, these cognitive shortcuts can quickly become oversimplified generalizations, sustaining damaging myths that obscure many populations' varied and complex realities.

Stereotypes can encourage bias, discrimination, and the loss of personal agency, regardless of their origins in racial, gender, religious, or other societal categories.

Stereotypes have a deep connection to historical, cultural, and institutional settings. Stereotypes are created and maintained in part by historical injustices, power imbalances, and social hierarchies. Racial stereotypes, for example, have a long history and are frequently linked to colonial narratives and the dehumanization of particular ethnic groups to legitimize oppression and exploitation. Similar to how patriarchal frameworks dictated strict roles and expectations for men and women, gender stereotypes have developed from them to perpetuate harmful norms that still exist in modern cultures.

Stereotypes are widely spread and actively challenged by the media, which is a potent cultural narrative builder. The way marginalized groups are portrayed in the media frequently perpetuates negative stereotypes by reflecting them and making them seem normal. In addition to restricting the possibilities open to members of marginalized populations, stereotypes serve to uphold negative biases, mold public opinion, and reinforce preexisting power disparities. Conversely, media can dispel prejudices by showcasing genuine stories, altering people's perspectives, and promoting inclusivity.

Stereotypes have far-reaching effects on people's opportunities, mental health, and self-esteem, among other aspects of their lives. Stereotype danger emphasizes the psychological toll stereotypes can have. It is a situation where members of stigmatized groups perform below expectations because they are afraid of confirming unfavorable perceptions. In addition, the persistence of preconceptions in academic and professional environments can result in skewed assessments, constrained career prospects, and the maintenance of structural disparities. Identifying and demolishing these prejudices is essential to establish settings in which people of all backgrounds can flourish.

In many countries, stereotypes about race and ethnicity are most prevalent because they are ubiquitous indicators of identity. Racial stereotypes reinforce negative prejudices that feed systemic racism since they are frequently firmly embedded in cultural narratives. For instance, perceptions about Black people might range from criminalization to exoticization, which can limit their chances and encourage prejudice. Asian groups may also face negative stereotypes that perpetuate negative beliefs about their talents and sense of belonging. These prejudices can range from the model minority myth to the idea that Asians are permanent outsiders.

Due to their deep historical roots in patriarchal customs, gender stereotypes impose strict demands on both men and women. Toxic masculinity is perpetuated by the idea that males should be stern, authoritative, and emotionless, which discourages men from expressing their vulnerability and emotions. However, preconceptions about women frequently depict them as emotional, nurturing, and less skilled in particular fields of work. Due to their restriction of possibilities and reinforcement of negative power dynamics, gender stereotypes play a part in the persistence of gender inequality.

Stereotyping based on sexual orientation and gender identity also feeds negative prejudices and further marginalizes LGBTQ+ people. For instance, negative stereotypes regarding homosexuality might range from portraying gay males as effeminate to misrepresenting bisexual people as promiscuous or indecisive. In addition to limiting the visibility of many identities within the LGBTQ+ community, these stereotypes also support prejudice, discrimination, and the denial of equal rights.

Stereotypes based on religion, which are frequently entwined with aspects of culture and race, help to sustain prejudice and discrimination. For example, there are misconceptions about Muslims that associate them with terrorism or depict Islam as fundamentally unjust. In addition to harming members of the Muslim community directly, these stereotypes also contribute to Islamophobia, societal fragmentation, and the perpetuation of false narratives about entire religious communities.

Individuals with impairments face prejudices that support ableism, creating unfavorable perceptions of their talents and restricting their possibilities. These prejudices, which stem from ignorance or sympathy, make people with disabilities feel marginalized and make it harder for them to participate in society, get an education, or find work. It is crucial to dispel these myths to promote an inclusive culture that honors every person's unique talents.

We must all work together to effectively combat stereotypes to promote understanding, compassion, and knowledge. As a potent instrument, education is essential for dispelling myths and encouraging critical thinking. From an early age, an inclusive curriculum that emphasizes the contributions and variety of experiences of excluded groups can change society's perceptions. Establishing cultures that celebrate diversity, dispel misconceptions, and advance inclusivity must be a top priority for educational institutions.

A further essential component in deconstructing stereotypes is media literacy. Media literacy initiatives can change public opinions by enabling people to question damaging narratives and critically examine how they are portrayed. It is equally essential to support a variety of voices and representations in the media. Media may be a force for good by promoting real tales that challenge preconceptions and encourage empathy and understanding across various viewers.

The systemic injustices that stereotypes sustain must be addressed through legislation and legislative efforts. Laws and rules against discrimination that encourage diversity and inclusion are essential instruments for breaking down preconceptions in several domains, such as public services, education, and the workplace. Furthermore, it is crucial to support diversity in leadership and decision-making roles to combat systematic prejudices and create workplaces that reflect humankind's diversity.

Advocacy and social movements are essential for dispelling myths and promoting cultural change. Movements like #MeToo, Black Lives Matter, and the struggle for LGBTQ+ rights are examples of how to challenge negative stereotypes, raise awareness, and drive structural improvements. These movements aid in deconstructing stereotypes and reconstructing societal narratives by elevating the voices of the oppressed.

It is the collective duty of individuals to confront and dispel preconceptions. To dispel stereotypes, it is imperative to have candid discussions, cultivate empathy, and face personal prejudices. Establishing forums for discussion, proactively pursuing varied viewpoints, and confronting detrimental presumptions all help foster an inclusive and understanding society.

In summary, dispelling stereotypes is a complex task that calls for coordinated efforts at the institutional, societal, and personal levels. By acknowledging the causes and effects of stereotypes, raising consciousness, and dedicating ourselves to empathy and education, we can destroy false narratives and work toward a more just and caring society. Beyond simple discourse, the need to confront stereotypes is a call to action, an undertaking to eliminate deeply rooted prejudices, and an affirmation of the richness of human diversity in all its manifestations.

CHAPTER III

Mindful Awareness

Introduction to Mindfulness

In the bustling tapestry of modern life, characterized by constant demands, rapid technological advances, and the perpetual race against time, mindfulness emerges as a beacon of serenity and self-discovery. With roots in antiquated contemplative techniques and a solid foundation in modern psychology and wellness discourse, mindfulness has crossed cultural barriers to become a game-changing tool in the fight for mental health. This section delves deeply into mindfulness practice, examining its history, central ideas, psychological foundations, real-world applications, and tremendous effects on individual and societal consciousness.

Mindfulness has its roots in Buddhist meditation techniques and comes from old contemplative traditions. The heart of this practice is captured by the Pali term "sati," which is generally translated as mindfulness. It refers to heightened awareness and non-judgmental- judgmental presence in the unfolding present. Mindfulness has developed within several contemplative traditions throughout the ages, each offering a distinctive viewpoint on developing an aware and sympathetic connection with the present moment. A significant change in the way the West views mental health and well-being has occurred in recent decades as a result of the mainstreaming of Mindfulness-Based Stress Reduction (MBSR) and other mindfulness-based interventions, thanks to the efforts of leaders such as Jon Kabat-Zinn.

The fundamental component of mindfulness is the development of an intentional, non-reactive awareness of one's thoughts, feelings, and sensations as they arise in the present moment. A quality of non-judgmental observation—allowing experiences to emerge without attachment or aversion—underpins this heightened awareness. Frequently utilized as an anchor, the breath acts as a center of attention, bringing people back to the present moment of their senses. The technique encourages people to make a significant perspective change and transition from a reactive, autonomic state to a deliberate, responsive one.

In terms of psychology, mindfulness has attracted much interest due to its profound effects on different aspects of mental health. According to neuroscience research, regular mindfulness practice alters the brain's structure, especially in regions related to attention, emotional control, and self-awareness. Studies using functional MRI show changes in the default mode network, emphasizing less self-referential thinking and more connectivity between attention and executive function-related brain areas.

Moreover, mindfulness has been included in treatment modalities like Mindfulness-Based Cognitive Therapy (MBCT), which prevents relapse in patients with recurrent depression by fusing mindfulness techniques with cognitive-behavioral techniques. An increasing amount of empirical research has confirmed the effectiveness of mindfulness in lowering stress and anxiety symptoms and enhancing psychological well-being in general. The practice of mindfulness, as evidenced by its application in various therapeutic contexts, highlights its promise as a comprehensive tool for addressing the complex interactions between the mind, emotions, and mental health.

Practically speaking, mindfulness is frequently taught through structured meditation techniques, such as body scan exercises, loving-kindness meditations, and concentrated attention on the breath. Through the gradual extension of the state of mindful awareness to everyday tasks, these organized practices offer a framework for people to hone and improve their mindfulness abilities. Informal mindfulness exercises that involve walking, mindful eating, or giving your whole attention to regular activities are good ways to incorporate mindfulness into daily life.

Mindfulness in interpersonal interactions goes beyond its application to personal well-being. Honest and compassionate relationships are facilitated by practicing non-judgmental attention and present-moment mindfulness. Active listening, being present, and providing meaningful answers are the hallmarks of mindful communication, which promotes peaceful relationships and reduces conflict. Mindfulness activities in the classroom have demonstrated the potential to improve students' focus, emotional control, and general well-being, all of which contribute to a productive learning environment.

There has been an increase in interest in mindfulness-based therapies to improve corporate culture and employee well-being in the workplace, which is frequently a furnace of stress and tight deadlines. Mindfulness programs aim to cultivate a mindful workplace culture, which ranges from quick workplace meditations to extensive interventions like Mindfulness-Based Stress Reduction (MBSR) and Mindful Leadership. According to research, practicing mindfulness at work can help employees become more resilient, focused, and satisfied with their jobs while lowering stress and burnout.

When used as a technique for personal development, mindfulness encourages people to delve deeper into their inner terrain. Beyond lowering stress, mindfulness promotes self-reflection and a kind, non-judgmental curiosity about one's feelings, ideas, and behavioral patterns. By encouraging people to accept the transience of experience, the practice builds resilience in facing life's unavoidable difficulties. A sense of connectivity is also fostered by practicing mindfulness, which makes one aware of the connections between one's well-being, the well-being of others, and the environment.

However, practicing mindfulness has its challenges.

Regular mindfulness practice may be hampered by modern life's demands, the ubiquitous distractions in the digital age, and cultural boundaries. The necessity for proper information and demystification of mindfulness is highlighted by skepticism and misconceptions around the practice, which range from seeing it as a mystical discipline divorced from reality to a passive escapist. Furthermore, the commercialization of mindfulness, detached from its moral underpinnings, raises questions about how its transformative potential can be compromised.

In summary, mindfulness offers a road to mental health,

self-discovery, and compassionate living, serving as a light of awareness in an increasingly hectic world. Its variety and ongoing importance are highlighted by its roots in ancient contemplative traditions, incorporation with current psychology, and applications in numerous parts of life. A profound journey that transcends time and place and cultivates an aware and harmonious relationship with the ever-unfolding present moment is what mindfulness invites people to as it continues to find its way into a variety of cultures and disciplines.

Mindful Breathing and Grounding Techniques

Mindfulness emerges as an anchor in the tumultuous currents of modern life, characterized by relentless demands and an unceasing barrage of stimuli. In this sanctuary, individuals can find respite and cultivate a profound connection with the present moment. Grounding exercises and mindful breathing are essential components of mindfulness practice. These tried-and-true methods give people a concrete route to emotional control, self- awareness, and improved well-being. To fully understand mindful breathing and grounding practices, this section will first examine their historical roots, the physiological and psychological mechanisms that support their effectiveness, and the various ways they can be used to navigate the complexity of the human experience.

The foundation of mindfulness practice, mindful breathing, has its roots in ancient contemplative traditions, especially in Buddhism. The mindfulness of breathing, or anapanasati, is a fundamental component of meditation techniques that encourage practitioners to focus on the feelings connected to each breath. The breath is a focal point for developing heightened awareness and a portal to the present moment. It is revered as a universal and ever-present rhythmic phenomenon. The popularization of mindful breathing in secular contexts was greatly aided by Jon Kabat-Zinn's Mindfulness-Based Stress Reduction (MBSR) program, which helped mindfulness move from its contemplative roots to modern psychology. This marked the beginning of an era in which the fusion of traditional wisdom and cutting-edge science revealed the practice's transformative power.

Developing a purposeful, non-judgmental awareness of the breath's inherent rhythm is the foundation of mindful breathing. People ground themselves in the instantaneity of the present moment by focusing on their breaths, in and out. The breath is a dependable focal point, a rhythmic dance that happens inside the body, reminding us that life is always in motion. The profound influence of mindful breathing is hidden by its simplicity, which provides a gateway to calmness and clarity amidst the noise of thoughts and outside stimuli.

The transforming potential of mindful breathing is demonstrated by its physiological impacts. Studies conducted in the domains of neurology and psychophysiology show that conscious breathing triggers the parasympathetic nervous system, commonly known as the "rest and digest" reaction. Heart rate, blood pressure, and cortisol levels—physiological markers of stress—drop due to this activation. Concurrently, conscious breathing raises vagal tone, an indicator of the vagus nerve's effectiveness in controlling the autonomic nervous system. These physiological alterations support a relaxed state that promotes stability and serenity.

In addition to its physiological impacts, mindful breathing significantly impacts emotional control and cognitive functions. The deliberate attention to the breath fosters a greater awareness of ideas and emotions as they arise. People become more emotionally and cognitively resilient when they watch these mental processes without reacting. By acting as a buffer against the mind's spontaneous responsiveness, mindful breathing enables people to respond to stimuli with intention instead of working on impulse. The therapeutic implications of mindfulness, especially in treating illnesses like anxiety, depression, and trauma, revolve around this cognitive shift.

In mindfulness, grounding practices act as extra anchors and are frequently used with mindful breathing. Grounding strategies are influenced by various sources, such as body-centered therapeutic approaches, dialectical behavior therapy (DBT), and somatic experiencing. Grounding oneself in the body's sensory sensations and the surrounding surroundings encourages people to establish a connection with the present moment. For those who find it challenging to be present just by mindful breathing or who are experiencing elevated levels of anxiety or dissociation, grounding is beneficial.

The 5-4-3-2-1 approach is a popular grounding technique in which participants list five senses—sight, touch, hearing, smell, and taste—and four senses—that they can identify. By focusing attention on the current environment, this sensory engagement fosters a sensation of presence. Another method of grounding is through conscious touch, such as putting a hand on one's chest or sensing the support of the earth beneath one's feet, or by using bodily sensations like experiencing the texture of an object or the tactile senses of one's clothing.

The effectiveness of grounding techniques is rooted in their capacity to cultivate a mental-physical connection that grounds people in the here and now. People can alleviate feelings of instability and safety by focusing on their sensory experiences instead of ruminating or worrying thoughts. Re-establishing a person's connection to the material parts of their experience, grounding is a countermeasure to dissociation, a condition in which people feel cut off from their bodies or the surrounding environment.

The harmonious fusion of grounding methods and mindful breathing improves the depth and adaptability of mindfulness practice. By combining these techniques, people can navigate the intricacies of their inner terrain and develop a comprehensive approach to self-awareness and present. These methods are also easy to use and accessible, which makes them valuable tools that can be integrated into daily life and provide brief breaks for rest and renewal in the middle of a busy day.

Applications of grounding exercises and mindful breathing go well beyond personal health to encompass many aspects of human existence. By implementing these strategies, educational settings can foster conditions that are favorable to learning by improving students' focus, attention, and emotional regulation. By promoting employee well-being, resilience, and creativity, the integration of mindfulness practices enhances the workplace, which is frequently a furnace of stress and demands. Anxiety, depression, and chronic pain therapies, as well as trauma-informed therapy, all include mindful breathing and grounding exercises as essential elements.

These techniques also have applications in interpersonal interactions, acting as stimulants for connection, empathy, and efficient communication. The quality of encounters is transformed by mindful communication based on the concepts of present and non-reactivity. The development of mindful listening, in which people listen intently and without passing judgment, enhances comprehension and fosters real connections. The integration of mindfulness practices in couples therapy is known to improve relational dynamics by promoting mutual awareness, reducing reactivity, and establishing compassionate communication spaces.

One of the most critical aspects of the use of mindful breathing and grounding techniques in trauma-informed treatment is their integration. Trauma frequently impairs a person's sense of safety and connection to the present moment, regardless of whether it results from recent or chronic hardship. Re-establishing a sense of stability, controlling intense emotions, and re-establishing a connection with one's body can all be achieved through the gentle process of mindfulness practices. These techniques are beneficial for trauma survivors since they are non-intrusive and provide tools for empowerment and self-control.

Nonetheless, there are several possible drawbacks to using grounding exercises and conscious breathing. These techniques may initially be overwhelming or distressing for people who have experienced trauma or who have specific mental health issues. The introduction of mindfulness must be done sensitively and under the supervision of qualified specialists in therapeutic settings. Furthermore, because mindfulness practices are personalized, it's essential to have a sophisticated awareness of each person's particular requirements, preferences, and cultural context to ensure the practices are applicable and approachable.

Practicing mindful breathing and grounding exercises can open doors to profound self-discovery, emotional control, and improved well-being. These activities provide a haven for people navigating the difficulties of contemporary life, a break from the never-ending streams of consciousness and outside stimuli. Their continued significance is shown by their roots in antiquated contemplative traditions, their incorporation into modern psychology, and a wide range of applications in many contexts. People discover periods of quiet and a deep connection to the constantly changing present through the subtle dance of mindful breathing and anchoring. This is an invitation to accept the entirety of the human experience with awareness, compassion, and a grounded sense of presence.

Applying Mindfulness to Anger Recognition and Response

In the intricate landscape of human emotions, anger is a potent force—an instinctual response rooted in the depths of our evolutionary history. Anger is a common and natural human emotion, but there are many different ways it can be expressed and what effect it has. With its origins in antiquated contemplative practices and a modern psychological rebirth, mindfulness provides a revolutionary method for comprehending, identifying, and handling anger. This section explores the origins of anger, the psychological processes involved, and the valuable applications of mindfulness in developing a more compassionate and skillful relationship with this complex emotion. It also explores how mindfulness can be applied to recognizing and responding to anger.

Anger has evolved from survival instincts and is frequently seen as a fundamental and protective emotion. The fight-or-flight reaction in the body is triggered in response to perceived threats or injustices, priming the person to react appropriately. Although our predecessors found that this natural reaction helped them deal with physical dangers, modern society's intricate social systems necessitate a more adaptive and nuanced response to rage. Anger can negatively impact one's general well-being, interpersonal relationships, and mental and physical health if it is unchecked or unmanaged. The first step to using anger's energy constructively is realizing and comprehending its complex nature.

The foundation of mindfulness practice is cultivating awareness, which is the first step in applying mindfulness to anger. Those who practice mindfulness are encouraged to examine their ideas, feelings, and physical experiences with an open-minded, instantaneous awareness. When it comes to anger, this means learning to identify when anger is about to happen, seeing how it shows up in the body and mind, and comprehending the underlying patterns and triggers. Raising awareness of the current moment enables people to stop the automatic reaction frequently linked to rage, making room for thoughtful and intelligent replies.

An essential mindfulness technique is mindful breathing, which acts as a stabilizing force in identifying and controlling anger. The breath becomes the center of attention since it is a constant and rhythmic part of who we are. The practice is to focus on the breath, notice how it naturally flows, and allow the breath to be a source of stability and grounding when anger emerges. In addition to breaking the vicious cycle of rage, this deliberate attention to the breath also triggers the parasympathetic nerve system, which aids in relaxation and emotional control. People can use mindful breathing as a practical strategy to control their emotions and make room for a more thoughtful reaction.

People who practice mindfulness are also encouraged to investigate the underlying ideas and viewpoints that give rise to feelings of anger. By engaging in mindfulness meditation, people can explore the stories and thought patterns linked to anger, leading to a better comprehension of its causes. This self-examination sheds light on the expectations, conditioned reactions, and interpretations that might exacerbate anger and open the door to a more discerning and understanding interaction with the underlying feelings. Acknowledging the cognitive distortions that frequently accompany rage allows people to question and reframe harmful thought patterns, which helps create a more realistic and balanced viewpoint.

To cultivate mindfulness in recognizing rage, one must accept the whole range of emotions without passing judgment. Acknowledging that anger is a normal and valid part of the human experience, mindfulness encourages people to name and validate their feelings just like any other emotion. People are less likely to repress or reject their anger when they approach it with inquiry and self-compassion when they adopt a non- judgmental mindfulness position. People can examine the subtleties of rage and distinguish between constructive outbursts and healthy manifestations of assertiveness by using this tolerant and open-minded approach.

In the area of interpersonal relations, mindfulness is equally crucial, especially when it comes to communicating and expressing anger. Relationships inevitably involve arguments and confrontations, and rage might surface due to perceived threats or boundary violations. People who practice mindfulness can better face interpersonal situations with composure and centering themselves. People can practice active listening, develop empathy, and react to people intentionally rather than reactively by integrating mindfulness into their conversations. Being present in the discussion, putting judgment aside, and creating a sincere interest in the thoughts and feelings of others are all components of mindful communication.

Apart from identifying rage, mindfulness enhances adept reactions by promoting emotional control. By practicing mindfulness, people can see how their emotions come and go without feeling overwhelmed or in control. Being more conscious of the current moment allows people to react to anger more intelligently, acting by their moral principles instead of acting on impulse. Particularly in those who are prone to recurring episodes of rage or violence, mindfulness-based therapies, such as Mindfulness-Based Cognitive Therapy (MBCT), have shown efficacy in reducing anger reactivity and improving emotional regulation.

Additionally, the idea of the "mindful pause"—a deliberate period of introspection before reacting angrily—is introduced by mindfulness. People can take a step back from habitual responses during this pause, which helps them see the issue more clearly. During the attentive pause, one should inhale deeply, pay attention to one's body's feelings, and weigh the possible outcomes of various actions. People can select a response that aligns more with their beliefs and long-term well-being thanks to this deliberate halt in the automatic reaction cycle.

Mindfulness to deal with rage goes beyond personal application to the institutional and cultural levels. Mindfulness-based therapies have been created to address anger-related concerns in therapeutic contexts, such as Mindfulness-Based Anger Management (MBAM). These programs give people valuable tools for identifying, controlling, and communicating anger through mindfulness and cognitive-behavioral techniques. Additionally, programs dealing with anger in educational settings have incorporated mindfulness, providing a comprehensive approach to emotional intelligence and conflict resolution for instructors and students.

Although mindfulness to address anger has a lot of potential, there are some possible drawbacks. At first, people can find it challenging to watch anger without becoming absorbed, or they could object to embracing anger without passing judgment. Furthermore, because instinctive reactions are deeply rooted, rewiring them might take persistent and focused exercise. People who have experienced trauma in the past may find mindfulness difficult in therapeutic settings; thus, they should seek the assistance of qualified specialists and make adjustments based on trauma theory. It is also crucial for mindfulness practices to be sensitive to cultural differences since cultural backgrounds can affect how mindfulness approaches to anger are understood and accepted.

To sum up, incorporating mindfulness in identifying and handling anger presents a significant and revolutionary method for managing the intricacies of this potent feeling. With its origins in modern psychology and ancient wisdom, mindfulness gives people the skills to control their emotions, develop awareness, and react to anger with compassion and intention.

By practicing mindfulness in interpersonal interactions, accepting the present moment, and cultivating a non-judgmental attitude, people can wisely and skillfully negotiate the complex terrain of rage. As mindfulness makes its way into educational curricula, therapeutic interventions, and public attitudes about anger, it urges people to travel on a path of self-exploration, emotional fortitude, and compassionate interaction with the ever-evolving currents of human experience.

CHAPTER IV

Compassionate Communication

The Power of Empathetic Listening

In the intricate dance of human connection, a profound and transformative force exists — empathetic listening. Rooted in the empathic capacity to truly understand and resonate with another person's experience, compassionate listening transcends the superficiality of mere hearing, forging a deep and authentic connection between individuals. This section examines the power of empathic listening and its psychological underpinnings, transforming effects on interpersonal relationships, emotional health, and the fabric of societal harmony.

The foundation of empathic listening is empathy, a complex and varied phenomenon involving the capacity to comprehend and experience another person's feelings. Although it is a fundamental feature of human nature, each person's expression is unique and influenced by social, cultural, and developmental circumstances. By actively and attentively engaging with another person's story, empathic listening harnesses the essence of empathy. Empathetic listening is a holistic and immersive experience that considers verbal and non-verbal indicators, emotional nuances, and the unsaid layers under speech's surface. This contrasts with passive hearing, which is the reception of auditory data.

The cornerstones of presence and attunement form the basis of empathic listening. Being present in the conversation, both physically and intellectually, is necessary for empathetic listening. It entails putting aside preconceived notions, developing genuine curiosity, and being willing to see the world from the perspective of others. Listeners with empathy can discern the speaker's emotional rhythm and minute variations in tone, body language, and underlying feelings underlying the story. The speaker can feel seen, heard, and validated in their own human experience when there is a visceral and intuitive connection made possible by this attunement that transcends the words expressed.

The complex dance between emotion and thought that underlies empathic listening is revealed by the psychological processes that support it. According to neuroscientific research, listening with empathy stimulates parts of the brain linked to social cognition and emotional processing. Mirror neurons facilitate empathetic resonance, a neural mirroring system in the brain that enables people to feel other people's emotions through a virtual experience. Between the speaker and the listener, this brain dance builds a bridge that fosters a shared emotional experience that goes beyond the bounds of individual subjectivity.

Furthermore, listening with empathy is reciprocal, fostering emotional intelligence, which is the capacity to identify, comprehend, and control one's emotions while navigating those of others. Empathetic listening helps people become more conscious of their feelings and understand the various emotional environments that other people are in. This mutual understanding-building process develops emotional receptivity and lays the groundwork for genuine and deep partnerships.

The transforming power of empathic listening reveals its impact on human interactions in a profoundly meaningful way. In intimate and mutually understanding relationships, whether friendships love partnerships, or family ties, empathic listening is essential. It establishes a relational environment in which people feel appreciated for the depth of their emotional experiences and welcomed for who they are. Being genuinely understood and heard fosters vulnerability, trust, and a feeling of our shared humanity. Misunderstandings are cleared up, disagreements are resolved, and the seeds of real connection are planted in the furnace of compassionate listening.

Empathetic listening is shown to be essential to counseling and psychotherapy in therapeutic settings. Equipped with the ability to listen with empathy, therapists establish a therapeutic relationship that allows clients to feel comfortable enough to express their deepest feelings and thoughts. The therapist's attentive listening skills and sympathetic comprehension of the client's story lay the foundation for healing and self- discovery. In therapy, listening with empathy is more than just a technique; it's a therapeutic approach that conveys sincere concern, deference, and unwavering positive regard, creating an atmosphere that supports the client's development and well-being.

Listening with empathy extends beyond personal connections and strengthens the bonds of understanding and peace in society. Empathetic listening creates empathy across social, cultural, and ideological divisions by bridging dissimilar experiences in the enormous tapestry of diverse views. People actively contribute to the destruction of stereotypes, the lessening of prejudice, and the development of a society that is more inclusive and compassionate by making an effort to learn the stories of others. Building bridges, fostering social cohesiveness, and fostering group development are all facilitated by empathic listening.

Empathetic listening's transforming effect on emotional well-being is evidence of its importance for resilience and mental health. Emotional processing and regulation can benefit therapeutically from telling one's story and receiving sympathetic understanding. People who have a sense of being acknowledged and understood are more adept at navigating the intricacies of their feelings, which lessens the weight of emotional suffering. Regardless of the setting—formal counseling or informal support—empathetic listening helps to improve psychological well-being, reduce feelings of isolation, and validate emotional experiences.

Intentional activities that go beyond basic techniques are necessary to cultivate empathy in listening, with an emphasis on genuine connection and sincerity. Empathetic listening begins with active listening, focusing entirely on the speaker, keeping eye contact, and communicating interest through verbal and nonverbal indicators. Going one step further, reflective listening involves the listener summarizing or paraphrasing the speaker's comments to ensure that their point of view has been understood correctly.
Developing curiosity, or a sincere desire to comprehend the nuances of another person's perspective, is another aspect of empathetic listening. This curiosity goes beyond the text and explores the emotional terrain that supports the story. Establishing a welcoming and secure environment for candid conversation can be facilitated by asking open-ended questions, looking for clarification, and sincerely showing a wish to learn.

With its focus on nonjudgmental observation and present-moment awareness, mindfulness is a natural ally in empathic listening. Being mindfully present entails focusing all of one's attention on the current situation, putting judgment aside, and practicing an open-minded attitude toward whatever comes up. When listening with empathy, mindfulness enables listeners to be present with the speaker and focus on the story's subtleties without being distracted by their thoughts or past judgments.

Developing empathic listening skills also takes a willingness to set aside one's agenda, prejudices, and presumptions. Metaphorically speaking, being able to put oneself in another person's shoes requires being receptive to viewpoints that may differ from one's own. This openness to empathy recognizes the subjectivity of personal experiences and that comprehension does not always equate to agreement. Holding space for a range of opinions, accepting the discomfort of ambiguity, and appreciating the intrinsic complexity of the human experience are all components of empathic listening.

The difficulties that come with listening with empathy result from the emotional openness and vulnerability it involves. It can be uncomfortable for the listener to navigate the emotional terrain of others; it can bring up unresolved issues or cause empathic pain. In addition, the listener could struggle with the want to push their own opinions, provide quick fixes, or relate personal tales—tendencies that take attention away from the speaker's experience. These difficulties draw attention to the subtlety of sympathetic listening and emphasize the value of constant self-awareness, reflective practice, and, when required, requesting assistance to manage the emotional intricacies involved.

As a result, in the complex dance of human relationships, empathic listening proves to be a powerful force that cuts beyond communication barriers and fosters genuine, deep connections. This transforming activity, which has its roots in empathy, transcends beyond the technical aspects of hearing and encompasses the domains of emotional resonance, comprehension, and shared humanity. In interpersonal interactions, therapeutic alliances, or the more prominent social cohesion framework, attentive listening guides compassionate involvement. Its ripple effects penetrate people's mental health, the fabric of interpersonal relationships, and the fabric of societal understanding. The depth of the human experience emerges in the stillness of authentic listening, paving the way for relationships, healing, and the harmonious interplay of many voices in the vast orchestra of life.

Expressing Emotions Constructively

In the intricate tapestry of human experience, emotions weave a complex and nuanced narrative, serving as the vibrant hues that paint the canvas of our lives. Central to this emotional landscape is the skill of expressing emotions constructively—an art that transcends the realms of mere verbal articulation to encompass a holistic understanding, regulation, and communication of the rich tapestry of feelings. An in-depth examination of the psychological foundations, the importance of emotional intelligence, and valuable techniques for negotiating the delicate dance of expressing emotions in ways that promote real connections, self-awareness, and general well-being are all covered in this section.

As essential elements of the human experience, emotions are complex and dynamic. They act as messengers, delivering critical information about our wants, needs, and reactions to the outside environment. The deliberate and purposeful transmission of these inner states to promote emotional well-being, build interpersonal relationships, and advance personal development is known as constructive emotional expression. Constructive emotional expression is a sophisticated talent that combines self-awareness, regulation, and efficient communication, in contrast to emotional expression as a chaotic outpouring of feelings.

Emotional intelligence is the fundamental component of constructive emotional expression. It is the capacity to identify, comprehend, regulate, and utilize one's emotions while negotiating those of others. Emotional intelligence, which has its roots in the groundbreaking research of psychologists Peter Salovey and John Mayer and was made public by Daniel Goleman, emphasizes the significance of emotional literacy as a vital component of social and personal competency. Constructive emotional expression demonstrates high emotional intelligence, which includes recognizing and appropriately categorizing emotions, comprehending the variables impacting emotional reactions, and expressing feelings in ways that advance understanding.

Self-awareness, or having a close understanding of one's emotional terrain, is the first step in constructively expressing emotions. This entails having the capacity to recognize and categorize emotions as they emerge, differentiate between subtle emotional nuances, and investigate the underlying causes of emotional reactions. Beyond the apparent expressive surface, self-awareness includes a deeper comprehension of the underlying values, beliefs, and personal experiences that influence emotional experiences. People with a high level of self-awareness can move across the complex dynamic landscape with curiosity, compassion, and an open mind.

Constructive emotional expression, as it pertains to emotional regulation, is the ability to control and direct emotions in a manner consistent with one's ideals and long-term welfare. Controlling one's emotions involves acknowledging and using adaptive strategies to manage them, not rejecting or repressing them. This regulation's foundation is mindfulness, an attitude of nonjudgmental observation and present-moment awareness. Mindfulness fosters thoughtful and productive expression of feelings by enabling intentional emotional responses instead of reactive behavior. Developing coping mechanisms, stress reduction methods, and a range of adaptive reactions to different emotional intensities are all included in the concept of emotional regulation.

Constructive emotional expression relies heavily on effective communication. Conveying one's internal states in a clear, assertive, and context- and other-aware manner is all part of constructive emotional communication. Assertiveness, a communication style that respects one's own needs and limits while acknowledging and validating the needs of others, is the foundation of this talent. Transceasing passive or hostile communication and constructive emotional expression provides a middle ground that encourages genuine relationships and candid conversation. Emotionally charged vocabulary, tone of voice, and timing play a part in how healthy emotions are communicated and received, fostering a respectful and empathetic atmosphere.

Effective communication of emotions is essential when it comes to interactions with other people. The resilience and quality of relationships are enhanced by the capacity to constructively express feelings, whether in friendships, romantic engagements, familial ties, or professional contacts. Constructive emotional expression is crucial in conflict resolution by promoting mutual understanding and cooperative problem-solving. While expressing negative emotions, like irritation or disappointment, presents chances for development and resolution, sharing positive feelings, like joy, thanks, and affection, forges connection links. Constructive emotional expression is reciprocal, which improves the vibrant atmosphere in relationships by fostering places for shared emotional experiences, empathy, and vulnerability.

Constructive emotional expression is an essential part of the counseling process in therapeutic settings. Equipped with a profound comprehension of emotional dynamics, therapists assist clients in examining and expressing their feelings lucidly and understanding ably. The openness and trust that define the therapeutic partnership give clients a secure environment to describe a wide range of emotions without fear of being judged. In addition to verbal communication, nonverbal cues, creative modalities, and the investigation of embodied sensations are examples of constructive emotional expression in therapy. Through this process, clients gain resilience and competence in navigating their dynamic landscapes and improved self-awareness and emotional literacy.

Cultural factors are significant in the complex understanding of healthy emotional expression. Communication techniques, cultural conventions, and passionate beliefs influence people's interpretations and expressions of emotions. While some cultures emphasize more overt and expressive expressions of emotions, others may place more significance on emotional reserve and indirect communication. Constructive emotional expression acknowledges and respects these cultural differences, and that appropriateness varies depending on the situation. Emotional expression that is cross- culturally competent requires attention to these subtleties, acceptance of other expressive expression styles, and knowledge of the cultural influences that shape emotional experiences.

A practical approach to fostering healthy emotional expression combines introspection, effective communication, and incorporating mindfulness into day-to-day activities. For instance, journaling offers a quiet, reflective setting where people can examine and express their feelings. In addition to improving self-awareness, this written expression can be used to arrange ideas and obtain focus before speaking with someone. Through developing a serene and centered presence and creating a space for non-reactive awareness, mindful activities like meditation and deep breathing exercises help with emotional regulation.

Alternative channels for healthy emotional expression are provided by expressive arts treatments, which include practices like dance/movement therapy, music therapy, and art therapy. These methods give people creative and nonverbal ways to express and explore feelings. Making art, playing music, or expressing oneself through movement can provide deep insights into emotional experiences that are difficult to describe fully. The vibrant worlds inside and outside of oneself are connected through creative expression.

Constructive emotional expression is enhanced by mindful communication skills, which are based on the ideas of empathy, active listening, and assertiveness. Sustaining judgment, focusing entirely on the speaker, and communicating participation via verbal and nonverbal indicators are all components of active listening. Mutual comprehension is further promoted via reflective listening, in which the listener summarizes or paraphrases the speaker's remarks to ensure understanding. Furthermore, assertiveness training gives people the skills to properly and effectively communicate their feelings, stand up for what they need, and be receptive to other people's viewpoints.

Difficulties about the constructive expression of emotions might originate from diverse origins. Recognizing and categorizing their feelings can be challenging, mainly when presented with a wide range of complicated emotions. Cultural standards or societal expectations restricting some emotional outbursts may make this problem even more difficult. Furthermore, people may find it challenging to communicate their feelings honestly if they are afraid of being judged, rejected, or in disagreement. These difficulties highlight how crucial it is to establish safe spaces that affirm and normalize a range of emotional experiences to lessen the stigma attached to expressing emotions.

Finally, positive emotional expression is a dynamic and transforming ability that enhances the human experience. This skill, based on emotional intelligence, self- awareness, and effective communication, includes identifying, controlling, and communicating emotions in ways that promote general well-being, personal development, and harmonious relationships. Constructive emotional expression becomes a compass for people as they traverse the complex terrain of their emotions; it points them in the direction of genuine connections, self- discovery, and a deep engagement with the dynamic fabric of human experience. Emotions find resonance, relationships grow, and the human spirit flourishes in the rich hues of actual existence when constructive emotional expression is used.

Developing Healthy Communication Patterns

In the intricate dance of human relationships, communication is the bedrock upon which connections are built, sustained, and transformed. Developing healthy communication patterns is an art and a science, intertwining the emotional nuances of human interaction with the practical skills that underpin effective dialogue. This section thoroughly investigates the complex aspects of healthy communication, covering topics such as psychological dynamics, the value of active listening, the significance of non-verbal cues, and doable tactics for developing communication patterns that promote comprehension, empathy, and the health of relationships.

A thorough comprehension of the complex interactions between ideas, feelings, and the spoken or written word is essential to effective communication. Communication is a dynamic process that involves the expression and interpretation of meaning, molded by human views, attitudes, and emotional states. It is not just a transaction of information. Understanding that communication is inherently subjective creates the foundation for developing constructive habits that transcend language to encompass the whole range of human experience.

The development of self-awareness is a crucial component in the art of healthy communication. A thorough understanding of one's feelings, ideas, and communication preferences is necessary for self-awareness. It necessitates the capacity to consider the effects of one's words, the underlying assumptions guiding communication styles, and the emotional currents influencing the conversation. People with a high level of self-awareness are more adept at navigating the intricacies of communication; they can identify when their emotions may impact their behavior and modify their communication style accordingly.

Active listening is a critical component of constructive communication styles, allowing for comprehension, empathy, and connection. Active listening is more than just hearing what is being said; it's a dynamic interaction in which the listener pays close attention, sets aside preconceived notions, and communicates understanding through spoken and nonverbal cues. Asking clarifying questions, demonstrating empathy, and paraphrasing or summarizing the speaker's remarks to ensure understanding are all part of the skill of active listening. People can express that they are totally present and sincerely interested in the thoughts and feelings of others by actively listening to each other.

Body language, tone of voice, and facial expressions are critical non-verbal clues in effective communication. Studies indicate that a significant amount of communication occurs through nonverbal means, highlighting the significance of coordinating verbal and nonverbal clues to achieve successful communication. Nonverbal cues provide depth to meaning by revealing information about the speaker's sincerity, the relationship's overall dynamics, and the communication's emotional tone. A more complex and genuine communication can be achieved by becoming aware of one's non-verbal clues and listening to others.

Healthy communication styles become essential for intimacy, trust, and mutual development in relationships. The Gottman Institute emphasizes the value of positive communication in happy partnerships. The institute is well-known for its studies on marital stability and divorce prediction. The Gottman model states that happy couples communicate well by expressing affection and admiration, demonstrating affection and appreciation, and resolving disagreements with mutual respect. Communication serves as a medium for more than just information sharing; it also facilitates the expression of love, the resolution of conflicts, and the joint construction of meanings.

The development of healthy patterns is presented with opportunities and problems by the effects of technology on communication. The emergence of digital communication platforms has broadened the range of interpersonal relationships by facilitating real-time experience sharing and distant connections. But the simplicity of digital communication also comes with drawbacks, like tone misreading, miscommunication, and the tendency to rely too much on brief, frequently unclear messages. Incorporating active listening and empathy into virtual exchanges, acknowledging the medium's limitations, and practicing mindfulness in text-based conversations are all important aspects of fostering healthy communication habits in the digital age.

People can cultivate various skills and habits in their daily interactions as part of practical techniques for creating and maintaining healthy communication patterns. To communicate mindfully, one must suspend habitual reactions, respond to communication with intention rather than reactivity, and bring a nonjudgmental awareness to the current moment. This approach lowers the possibility of misunderstandings, makes room for intelligent answers, and promotes transparency and understanding.

Using "I" statements instead of "you" denotes a change in communication style toward individual accountability and assertiveness. "I" statements convey the speaker's needs, wants, and feelings without passing judgment or blaming others. This methodology fosters openness, diminishes defensiveness, and encourages cooperative investigation of mutual viewpoints. For instance, having a meaningful conversation is more conducive to saying, "I feel overwhelmed when there's a lack of communication about our plans," in contrast to "You always make plans without consulting me."

Healthy communication practices incorporate conflict resolution as a necessary component, recognizing that conflicts and differences will inevitably arise in relationships. To resolve disputes positively, it is essential to follow the concepts of assertiveness, active listening, and empathy. Healthy conflict resolution calls for an openness to hearing other people's points of view, a readiness to compromise, and an emphasis on the matter rather than making personal attacks; establishing a courteous and secure environment for voicing divergent viewpoints aids in dispute resolution in ways that improve rather than damage relationships.

Culturally competent communication acknowledges and values the variety of ways that people from various cultural backgrounds express themselves and understand communication. Tolerance for emotional expressiveness, non-verbal clues, and direct or indirect communication preferences can all be influenced by cultural norms, communication styles, and the hierarchy. Curiosity, a readiness to learn about other communication modalities, and an openness to changing one's habits to promote cross-cultural understanding are necessary to develop cultural competence.

It can be not easy to establish healthy communication habits for several reasons. People may encounter obstacles, including fear of vulnerability, reluctance to communicate their feelings, or profoundly ingrained communication patterns from a previous life. Defensiveness, avoidance, or hostility might be symptoms of unhealthy communication patterns that were acquired in one's family of origin or previous relationships. In addition, outside stressors like job demands or life changes can affect communication dynamics and make it challenging to maintain good habits. To overcome these obstacles, one must be self-aware, engage in continual introspection, and be prepared to ask for help when necessary.

To sum up, mutual understanding, productive teamwork, and strong relationships all depend on healthy communication patterns. Healthy communication is based on self-awareness, assertiveness, and active listening. It embraces the complexity of the human experience and goes beyond just verbal exchanges. It entails handling disagreement with grace and empathy, cultural competency, and the dynamic interaction of verbal and nonverbal signs. When people set out to create healthy communication patterns, they also help create relational spaces where understanding grows, connection strengthens, and the human spirit comes alive in the harmonious interaction of real conversation.

CHAPTER V

Self-Reflection Exercises

Journaling Prompts for Exploring Anger Triggers

Embarking on a journey of self-discovery often involves peeling back the layers of our emotional landscape, and when it comes to anger, understanding its triggers can be a profound and transformative exploration. Writing in a journal is an effective technique that offers a private, secure environment for exploring the complexities of our feelings. This section explores several journaling exercises that help people discover what causes their anger, identify recurring themes, and better comprehend the emotions that give rise to this powerful force.

Start by thinking back to instances in the past where you felt angry. Give a detailed account of the situations, the people involved, and what made you angry. Take into account the emotion's strength and any impulsive responses. Writing in your journal about recent occurrences gives you a head start on comprehending the immediate triggers and environmental elements that fuel your rage. Look through your diary entries over an extended period to find any themes or patterns related to your anger. Are any particular circumstances, connections, or exchanges constantly angering you? Consider whether these tendencies have continued over time and if any themes or recurring themes connect different episodes of rage in your life.

Examine your early encounters with rage using childhood recollections. Think back to your childhood, the messages you were taught about anger, and how it was exhibited or repressed in your family. Writing in a journal about your early life events might reveal ingrained attitudes and taught anger management techniques. Determine what's causing your anger right now and what's causing it later. Write in your journal about the obvious things that make you angry, then explore the deeper feelings, unfulfilled desires, or underlying convictions that might be causing these things. Understanding the underlying reasons for anger might help one better understand the layers that lie behind its surface manifestation.

Examine the physical manifestations of rage. Describe your reactions to anger, such as tenseness, a faster heartbeat, or other physiological changes. Writing in your journal on the physical features of anger will help you become more aware of your body's signals and provide essential insights into how this emotion feels on the somatic level. Differentiate between outside factors and personal triggers that make you angry. Consider the structural elements, cultural norms, and societal expectations that might affect your emotional reactions. Writing in a journal about how social influences and personal triggers interact might help reveal the complex nature of rage.

Consider the ways that anger appears in your relationships. Note your interactions with loved ones, close friends, coworkers, or romantic relationships. Examine if relationship patterns regularly make you angry and investigate how power dynamics, communication styles, or unfulfilled expectations influence these patterns. Examine the thought processes and meanings you link with your anger. Examine the ideas, presumptions, or interpretations that come to mind when confronting situations that make you angry. Writing in a journal about your cognitive processes can reveal automatic thought patterns, false ideas, or cognitive distortions that influence your emotional reactions.

Examine the ways that your anger manifests in your conduct. Write in your journal how anger affects your behavior, manner of speaking, or choices. Examine your values and boundaries about anger. Think about any particular activities you engage in when you're angry. Think about the effects these behaviors have on you and others. Consider whether your anger is a sign of a breach of personal space or if it is consistent with your fundamental beliefs. Writing in your journal about how your beliefs and anger interact can help you identify when anger is a healthy way to set boundaries and when it might need more investigation.

Think about the ways you now manage your anger. Please write in your journal about the methods you use to control or release your anger, whether helpful or dangerous. Look into other coping strategies that support your mental health and give you healthier ways to let your anger out. Incorporate mindfulness into your journaling practice to investigate the function of present-moment awareness in controlling your anger. Write in your journal about your experiences using grounding exercises, mindful breathing, or other mindfulness approaches when confronted with events that make you angry. Consider how mindfulness has affected your capacity to react to anger more purposefully and mindfully.

While participating in these writing exercises, remember that the process is investigative and could develop gradually. Be curious and self-compassionate when responding to each provocation, realizing that it takes a journey to comprehend and change the complexity of rage. Maintaining a regular journal can be a helpful tool in this investigation, offering a contemplative environment for development, self-awareness, and building a more positive relationship with the complex web of human emotions.

Analyzing Past Anger Episodes

Embarking on the journey of self-discovery often entails navigating the complex terrain of our emotions, and few feelings carry as much intensity and potential for transformation as anger. Analyzing past anger episodes becomes a profound and reflective exploration, shedding light on the layers of emotion, triggers, and responses that shape our experiences. This section explores the nuances of examining previous instances of anger, leading readers through a contemplative process that reveals trends, provides new perspectives, and promotes a greater comprehension of the complex nature of rage.

Think back to the direct causes of previous outbursts of rage to start. Write in your journal about the precise things that happened or the words or deeds that set you off. Think about the situation, the people involved, and the strength of the feeling at that particular time. Knowing what external causes cause rage reactions can be started by analyzing immediate triggers. Examine the depth and emotional relevance of previous instances of rage. Think back on the intensity of your feelings, whether they were brief annoyances, brewing dissatisfaction, or exploding fury. Think about the emotional spectrum and how distinct underlying causes may correspond with different intensities. Dynamic intensity analysis reveals the various nuances of rage that permeate your experiences.

Analyze the trends when you compare angry episodes in various situations. Consider whether specific themes or triggers keep coming up in different spheres of your life, such as relationships, career, or personal struggles. By examining trends in various circumstances, you can learn more about the generality or specificity of your anger triggers and reactions. Examine the guiding principles and underlying assumptions that may have shaped your responses in previous instances of rage. Write in your journal about the ideas, presumptions, or beliefs that drove your emotional reactions. Consider whether your anger indicated a misalignment that needs further exploration or if it was in line with your basic values. Examining fundamental ideas reveals the mental terrain that molds your emotional encounters.

Think back on how previous outbursts of rage have affected your relationships. Think about how your outbursts of rage affected your relationships with loved ones, friends, coworkers, or romantic partners. Examine if specific communication or behavior patterns during rage involved the relationship problems. Examining how it affects relationships might provide important information about your anger's interpersonal aspects. Analyze the coping and anger management techniques you have used in the past. Consider whether your answers tended toward potentially destructive outlets or toward beneficial ones like going for solitude, practicing mindfulness, or exercising. Examining your coping mechanisms reveals possibilities for improvement and helps you assess the effectiveness of your present tactics.

Think back to the bodily experiences connected to previous moments of rage. Write in your journal about the physical signs of your anger, such as tenseness, a faster heartbeat, or other physiological reactions. Consider the bodily manifestation of rage and whether any biological indicators existed during several instances. Understanding the embodied features of rage better requires an analysis of physical feelings. Look into the idea that unmet demands caused previous outbursts of rage. Consider if your anger was a response to disappointed expectations, unfulfilled aspirations, or unsolved problems. Consider how recognizing and meeting these unfulfilled needs can affect how you handle anger in the future. Examining unfulfilled wants reveals the link between individual goals and outbursts of rage.

Analyze the cognitive evaluations and interpretations that influenced how you perceived what happened during previous episodes of rage. Write in your journal about any ideas or conclusions that came to mind during the pressure and affected your feelings. Examine if any cognitive distortions were at play and consider how changing your perspective could influence how you react in the future. Examining cognitive assessments helps one become more conscious of the thought processes involved in anger. Consider how previous outbursts of rage have affected your identity and sense of self. Think about whether the way you express your rage creates internal problems or if it fits with your self-concept. Examine if responding to angry episodes reflects the kind of person you want to be and how your identity's congruence or incongruence influences your emotional experiences.

Determine the lessons and opportunities for progress that can be drawn from previous instances of anger. Write in your journal about any realizations, viewpoint shifts, or behavioral changes that resulted from angry outbursts. Examine how these teachings fit into your current emotional development and self-discovery process. Taking stock of your potential for progress cultivates a revolutionary and forward-thinking outlook. Incorporate mindfulness exercises into your examination of previous instances of rage. Consider if you used any mindfulness practices during angry episodes, such as focused breathing or grounding exercises, or if they could have been helpful. Examine how mindfulness, which promotes present-moment awareness and non-reactive observation, could affect how you handle anger.

Approach the reflective process of reviewing previous outbursts of rage with an open mind, self-compassion, and a dedication to personal development. Realize that this inquiry aims to gain a sophisticated grasp of the complex tapestry of your emotional experiences, not to pass judgment on yourself. Individuals can receive insights that facilitate deliberate and conscious responses, transformative development, and the development of emotional well-being by carefully examining the strands of anger.

Setting Personal Goals for Anger Management

Embarking on the anger management journey is a profound commitment to self-awareness, growth, and emotional well-being. Setting personal goals becomes an integral aspect of this transformative process, providing a roadmap for individuals to navigate the complexities of their emotions and cultivate healthier responses to anger. This section examines the importance of setting personal goals for anger management to help people through a reflective journey that includes goal-setting, integrating mindfulness practices, creating healthy coping mechanisms, and encouraging long-lasting behavioral changes.

Defining objectives and identifying triggers are the first steps in creating a personal anger management goal. Think about the particular areas of your anger that you want to work on, such as the severity of your emotional outbursts, how often you become angry, or how it affects your relationships. Simultaneously, determine the triggers that elicit rage consistently. These triggers should include both direct stimuli and underlying patterns. Create focused and productive goal-setting by clarifying your triggers and objectives.

Incorporate mindfulness exercises into your anger management plans to develop a more acute awareness of yourself. The deliberate, nonjudgmental observation of one's experiences in the moment is critical to mindfulness. Make it a point to include mindfulness exercises in your everyday routine, such as body scans, mindful breathing, or meditation. By engaging in these activities, one can develop a deeper awareness of the feelings, ideas, and bodily sensations linked to anger and pause before acting on it.

Creating constructive coping strategies in place of harmful or ineffective responses is part of setting personal objectives for anger management. Determine the precise coping mechanisms that will help you achieve your goals.

Consider activities that encourage calmness, stress relief, and emotional control. This could be working out physically, doing deep breathing techniques, or reaching out for social support. Building a toolkit of good coping techniques gives you the advantage in handling events that make you angry.

Establish objectives to improve emotional control, emphasizing the growth of abilities to control the amount and duration of rage. Consider how dynamic control has affected your quest to manage your anger, and note any tactics that speak to you. This could be practicing cognitive reappraisal, becoming aware of the early warning signs of anger, or partaking in activities that encourage composure. Emotional regulation objectives support a more flexible and deliberate reaction to rage.

Acknowledge communication's role in controlling your anger and make plans to work on your communication abilities. Consider attending conflict resolution workshops, active listening classes, or assertiveness training as growth opportunities. Objectives in this area include developing honest and compassionate communication, understandably stating needs, and authoritatively expressing emotions. Improved communication abilities help to reduce escalation during angry episodes and promote more positive connections.

Incorporate objectives that promote perspective-taking and empathy, acknowledging that managing anger requires grasping other people's points of view. Consider instances where empathy could have helped to calm tension and make goals to practice it. In this field, objectives include actively weighing other viewpoints, listening, and developing empathy for other people's feelings. You may promote a more sympathetic and sophisticated attitude to interpersonal interactions by cultivating compassion.

If underlying problems cause recurrent problems with rage, think about establishing objectives linked to getting help from a therapist. Therapy offers a disciplined and encouraging setting for discovering the underlying reasons for anger, gaining understanding, and creating coping mechanisms. Establish goals for attending therapy sessions, working on self-reflection, and actively participating in the therapeutic process. Therapy that addresses underlying causes improves the depth and durability of anger control objectives.

Establish objectives to foster an upbeat emotional environment in your social and personal spheres. Think about how your emotional outbursts affect the relationships and the atmosphere. Objectives could be expressing thanks, bringing optimism into conversations, or creating a welcoming and affirming environment. You can reduce the possibility of an angry outburst by deliberately fostering a positive emotional environment.

Include objectives for monitoring your development and acknowledging accomplishments as you move through the anger management process. Create a framework for tracking how you react to rage, evaluating how well techniques work, and recognizing achievements. This category of goals includes regular self-evaluation, journaling about progress, and celebrating minor and significant victories. Monitoring your development gives you insightful feedback and supports the constructive adjustments you've made to your anger management strategy.

Establish objectives for continued education and development in the area of anger control. Recognize that you are always learning new things, and set goals to increase your knowledge and abilities. This could be reading books on controlling your anger, attending seminars or workshops, or looking for a mentor. Continuous learning goals encourage a proactive and flexible approach to managing anger at various stages of life.

Acknowledge the significance of developing endurance and forbearance when confronted with obstacles. As you acknowledge that there may be difficult times along the road to anger control, set goals to build resilience in the face of setbacks. Practice self-compassion by giving oneself room to develop and improve. An attitude that is more self-affirming and sympathetic toward the unavoidable highs and lows of the anger management process is enhanced by goals of resilience and patience.

Try establishing objectives linked to developing a network of people who understand and support your journey towards managing your anger. Determine who in your circle of friends, family, or support systems can provide empathetic understanding and helpful criticism. This domain may include objectives like informing your support system of your plans, getting their feedback, and encouraging accountability. Creating a network of allies strengthens your resolve to control your anger and offers a priceless source of support and direction.

To sum up, creating personal goals for controlling one's anger is a dynamic and empowering process that promotes emotional balance and well-being. These objectives function as benchmarks, guiding people toward deliberate and flexible ways to deal with anger while encouraging self-awareness and development. Setting goals should be approached compassionately as you begin this journey, understanding that transformation is slow. By carefully incorporating these objectives into your day-to-day activities, you set off on a journey that deals with anger and develops empathy, resilience, and a deep understanding of the complex web of emotions that make up your emotions.

CHAPTER VI

Building Emotional Intelligence

Recognizing and Nurturing Emotional Literacy

In the rich tapestry of human experience, emotions weave a profound narrative that shapes our perceptions, interactions, and personal growth. Central to this narrative is emotional literacy, the ability to recognize, understand, and express emotions with depth and nuance. This section explores the significance of acknowledging and nurturing emotional literacy, delving into the foundational components, the impact on various facets of life, and practical strategies for fostering a heightened awareness and intelligence in the realm of emotions.

Emotional literacy begins with the cultivation of self-awareness—a reflective journey into the intricate landscape of one's emotions. This involves identifying and labeling a wide range of emotions, from joy and excitement to sadness, anger, and fear. Self-awareness extends beyond the surface, inviting individuals to explore the subtleties of their emotional experiences, discerning the nuances between similar emotions, and understanding the interplay of multiple emotions at any given moment.

Furthermore, emotional literacy encompasses the aptitude for recognizing emotions in others—a skill often referred to as social awareness. This involves attuning to non-verbal cues, such as facial expressions, body language, and tone of voice, to decipher the emotions that others may be experiencing. Social awareness extends to empathy—the ability to understand and share the feelings of others, cultivating a connection that transcends verbal communication.

The impact of emotional literacy resonates across various domains of life, influencing personal well-being, relationships, communication, and even professional success. In personal well-being, individuals with high emotional literacy navigate the complexities of their emotions with greater ease. They are equipped to manage stress, cope with challenges, and maintain a resilient outlook, fostering a sense of emotional balance and harmony within themselves.

Emotional literacy becomes a linchpin for intimacy, understanding, and effective communication in relationships. Couples with high emotional literacy are better positioned to navigate conflicts, express their needs, and create a relational space where emotions are acknowledged and validated. Friendships, family dynamics, and professional relationships also benefit from the depth of understanding that emotional literacy brings, fostering a climate of trust, empathy, and authentic connection.

Communication, as a vehicle for human interaction, is profoundly influenced by emotional literacy. The ability to express emotions articulately, with clarity and authenticity, enhances communication effectiveness. Conversely, individuals with limited emotional literacy may need help to convey their feelings, leading to misunderstandings, unexpressed needs, and a diminished capacity for meaningful connection.

The workplace, too, is not immune to the impact of emotional literacy. Leaders with high emotional intelligence foster a positive organizational culture where employees feel seen, heard, and valued. Effective teamwork, conflict resolution, and adaptive decision-making are all influenced by the emotional intelligence of individuals within the professional sphere. Moreover, emotional literacy contributes to a workplace environment that recognizes and supports the emotional well-being of its members.

Practical strategies for recognizing and nurturing emotional literacy span a spectrum of intentional practices and mindset shifts. As a reflective tool, journaling provides a space for individuals to explore and articulate their emotions. Writing about daily experiences, significant events, and emotional responses cultivates self-awareness and deepens the connection to one's dynamic landscape. Mindfulness practices, such as meditation and mindful breathing, offer opportunities to observe emotions in the present moment without judgment, fostering a non-reactive awareness.

Engaging in open and honest conversations about emotions—both with oneself and with others—contributes to the development of emotional literacy. Creating a culture of emotional expression within relationships and communities encourages individuals to share their feelings, fostering mutual understanding and connection. Additionally, seeking feedback from trusted individuals can provide valuable insights into blind spots and areas for growth in emotional intelligence.

Educational initiatives that integrate emotional intelligence into curricula contribute to nurturing emotional literacy from an early age. Schools and educational institutions play a pivotal role in fostering emotional intelligence through programs that teach emotional regulation, empathy, and effective communication. These initiatives equip individuals with the foundational skills needed to navigate adulthood's complex, dynamic landscape.

Mindful reading and exposure to diverse narratives can also contribute to the development of emotional literacy. Whether fiction or non-fiction, literature offers glimpses into the myriad ways emotions are experienced and expressed. Characters in stories become mirrors, reflecting aspects of the reader's emotional journey and expanding their emotional vocabulary.

Moreover, fostering emotional literacy involves embracing a growth mindset—believing that emotional intelligence can be developed and refined over time. This mindset shift encourages individuals to view challenges as learning opportunities, seek feedback for continuous improvement, and approach emotions with a curiosity that transcends fixed notions. Acknowledging that emotional literacy is a lifelong journey promotes an ongoing commitment to self-discovery and growth.

In conclusion, recognizing and nurturing emotional literacy emerge as essential components of the human experience, shaping the quality of relationships, personal well-being, and societal interactions. This journey into the realm of emotions involves self-awareness, social awareness, and the ability to express and understand feelings with nuance. As individuals and communities prioritize the development of emotional literacy, they contribute to a world where empathy, understanding, and authentic connection form the foundation for a more harmonious and enriched existence.

Understanding the Connection Between Emotions and Behavior

In the intricate tapestry of human experience, emotions and behavior engage in a perpetual dance, each influencing and shaping the other in a complex interplay that defines our responses to the world. This section explores the profound connection between emotions and behavior, delving into the intricate ways in which our emotional landscape influences the choices we make, the actions we take, and the patterns we weave into the fabric of our lives.

Emotions, as the vibrant hues of the human psyche, serve as powerful guides, offering insights into our inner world and external interactions. They are the visceral responses to the ebb and flow of life, ranging from joy and love to anger, sadness, fear, and beyond. As integral components of the human experience, emotions function as messengers, conveying information about our needs and desires and the alignment of our experiences with our internal landscapes.

The connection between emotions and behavior is nuanced and multifaceted, encompassing a spectrum of responses that unfold in both conscious and subconscious realms. Conscious behaviors, rooted in deliberate choices and cognitive processing, often reflect the influence of emotions on decision-making. For instance, an individual experiencing the warmth of love may express affection through acts of kindness. At the same time, someone gripped by the intensity of anger may engage in assertive or aggressive behaviors to respond to perceived threats or injustices.

Conversely, subconscious behaviors, driven by automatic responses and deeply ingrained patterns, may unfold without conscious awareness of the emotional undercurrents. These automatic behaviors, often shaped by past experiences and learned responses, can become habitual reactions to specific emotional triggers. For example, an individual with a history of trauma may exhibit avoidance behaviors in response to situations that evoke feelings of fear or vulnerability, even if those emotions are not consciously acknowledged.

The relationship between emotions and behavior becomes particularly pronounced in moments of emotional arousal, where the intensity of feelings can act as a catalyst for action. Positive emotions, such as joy or excitement, may propel individuals toward engaging in activities that align with those emotions, contributing to a sense of vitality and fulfillment. On the other hand, if left unexamined, negative emotions can lead to behaviors aimed at alleviating discomfort, even if those behaviors are not conducive to long-term well-being.

Understanding the connection between emotions and behavior involves recognizing the role of cognitive processes in shaping our responses. Cognitive appraisal, evaluating situations and events through our beliefs, values, and past experiences, plays a pivotal role in determining the behavioral outcomes of emotional experiences. For instance, two individuals facing the same challenging situation may respond differently based on their unique cognitive appraisals and interpretations of the event.

The intricate dance between emotions and behavior is further illuminated by the concept of emotional regulation—the capacity to modulate and manage the intensity and expression of emotions. Effective emotional regulation allows individuals to respond to emotions in adaptive ways, choosing behaviors that align with long-term goals and values. In contrast, challenges in emotional regulation may lead to impulsive or maladaptive behaviors as individuals grapple with overwhelming emotions without the skills to navigate them effectively.

The connection between emotions and behavior is not confined to the individual level; it ripples through the fabric of interpersonal dynamics and societal structures. In relationships, emotional expressions become the currency through which individuals convey their needs, establish boundaries, and forge connections. The ability to recognize and respond to the emotions of others, often referred to as empathy, plays a crucial role in the quality of interpersonal interactions and the establishment of meaningful connections.

Moreover, the collective behaviors of societies and communities are shaped by the prevailing emotional climate—a confluence of shared values, attitudes, and the collective emotional experiences of its members. Societal norms, cultural expectations, and the response to collective challenges are all influenced by the emotional undercurrents that permeate the collective consciousness. The impact of this connection between emotions and behavior is evident in social movements, cultural shifts, and the dynamics of power and influence within societies.

Practical strategies for understanding and navigating the connection between emotions and behavior involve intentional practices that cultivate emotional intelligence. Emotional intelligence encompasses the ability to recognize, understand, and manage one's feelings, as well as the capacity to empathize with and navigate the emotions of others. Mindfulness practices like meditation and mindful breathing allow individuals to observe their feelings without immediate reactivity, fostering self-awareness and emotional regulation.

Therapeutic modalities, such as cognitive-behavioral therapy (CBT), provide individuals with tools to identify and challenge maladaptive thought patterns and behaviors rooted in distorted perceptions of reality. CBT empowers individuals to develop more adaptive responses to emotional triggers, promoting a greater alignment between emotions and behavior. Similarly, dialectical behavior therapy (DBT) emphasizes the integration of acceptance and change, offering skills for emotional regulation and interpersonal effectiveness.

Reflective practices like journaling facilitate a deeper understanding of the connections between emotions and behavior. Regularly documenting emotional experiences, behavioral responses, and the associated thoughts and interpretations provides individuals with a tangible record that can unveil patterns, triggers, and areas for growth. This reflective process contributes to the development of emotional literacy—an awareness and fluency in the language of emotions.

Education and awareness initiatives that promote emotional intelligence in schools, workplaces, and communities contribute to a broader understanding of the connection between emotions and behavior. Incorporating emotional intelligence into educational curricula equips individuals with the skills to navigate the complexities of emotions, make informed decisions, and foster positive interpersonal relationships.

In conclusion, the connection between emotions and behavior weaves a dynamic and intricate tapestry that shapes the essence of our humanity. The dance between feelings and behavior unfolds in the vast expanse of individual experiences, interpersonal interactions, and societal dynamics. Recognizing and understanding this connection involves a journey of self-discovery, emotional regulation, and the cultivation of empathy. This journey illuminates the path toward more intentional and authentic ways of engaging with the rich palette of human emotions.

Developing Emotional Regulation Skills

In the intricate dance of human experience, emotions surge and recede like waves, shaping our perceptions, decisions, and interactions with the world. At the heart of this dynamic interplay lies the concept of emotional regulation—a set of skills that empowers individuals to navigate the ebb and flow of their emotions with grace and intention. This section explores the profound significance of developing emotional regulation skills, delving into the foundational components, the impact on mental well-being, relationships, and daily functioning, and practical strategies for cultivating a harmonious relationship with one's emotional landscape.

Emotional regulation involves the conscious and adaptive management of one's emotions—an art that requires self-awareness, mindfulness, and a repertoire of coping strategies. At its core, developing emotional regulation skills begins with the cultivation of self-awareness—the ability to recognize and understand one's emotional experiences. This foundational skill serves as a compass, guiding individuals through the landscape of their feelings and fostering a conscious engagement with the emotions that arise in various situations.

As a critical component of emotional regulation, mindfulness invites individuals to observe their emotions without immediate judgment or reactivity. Mindfulness practices, such as meditation, mindful breathing, or body scans, allow individuals to anchor themselves in the present moment, creating a buffer between the surge of emotions and impulsive reactions. The cultivation of mindfulness enhances the capacity for non-reactive awareness, allowing individuals to respond to emotions with intention rather than succumbing to automatic and potentially maladaptive behaviors.

The impact of developing emotional regulation skills reverberates through mental well-being, influencing an individual's capacity to manage stress, cope with challenges, and maintain a resilient outlook. Emotional regulation protects against the detrimental effects of chronic stress, contributing to psychological flexibility and adaptive coping. Individuals adept at regulating their emotions are better equipped to navigate life's inevitable ups and downs, fostering a sense of emotional balance and well-being.

In relationships, emotional regulation plays a pivotal role in interpersonal dynamics. The ability to regulate one's emotions contributes to effective communication, conflict resolution, and the establishment of healthy boundaries. In intimate relationships, partners with solid emotional regulation skills create a relational space where emotions are acknowledged, validated, and navigated with mutual understanding. Moreover, emotional regulation enhances empathy—the capacity to understand and share the feelings of others—fostering deeper connections and attunement in interpersonal interactions.

Emotional regulation skills profoundly influence daily functioning, whether in personal or professional contexts. In the workplace, individuals who can effectively regulate their emotions navigate challenges with composure, make informed decisions, and contribute to a positive organizational culture. Emotional regulation enhances problem-solving abilities, communication effectiveness, and the capacity to work collaboratively with others. In personal pursuits, from goal-setting to decision-making, emotional regulation is a guiding force, aligning actions with long-term objectives and values.

Practical strategies for developing emotional regulation skills encompass a spectrum of intentional practices and mindset shifts. Cognitive-behavioral therapy (CBT), a therapeutic modality that integrates cognitive restructuring and behavioral strategies, offers individuals tools to identify and challenge maladaptive thought patterns associated with emotional distress. CBT empowers individuals to develop more adaptive responses to emotional triggers, fostering a greater alignment between emotions and behavior.

Beyond their role in self-awareness, mindful practices provide a platform for cultivating emotional regulation. Mindful breathing exercises, for instance, offer individuals a tangible technique to anchor themselves in the present moment during emotional arousal. By redirecting attention to the breath, individuals create a pause that disrupts the automatic cascade of emotions and allows space for intentional responses.

Emotion-focused coping strategies, such as expressive writing or creative outlets, provide avenues for processing and expressing emotions constructively. Engaging in activities that allow the externalization of emotions through journaling, art, or physical outlets contributes to a sense of catharsis and emotional release. These strategies empower individuals to channel the energy of emotions into creative and purposeful endeavors.

Social support and connection play a crucial role in emotional regulation. They share emotions with trusted individuals, whether friends, family, or a support group, providing a relational context for validation and understanding. In the presence of empathetic listeners, individuals often experience relief, and verbalizing emotions contributes to integrating cognitive and emotional processes.

Mindful awareness of physiological sensations associated with emotions is another avenue for developing emotional regulation skills. Body-focused practices, such as progressive muscle relaxation or body scans, allow individuals to attune to the physical manifestations of emotions. By cultivating awareness of bodily cues, individuals gain insights into the somatic dimensions of their emotional experiences, facilitating a more holistic approach to emotional regulation.

Education and awareness initiatives disseminate information and tools for developing emotional regulation skills. Workshops, seminars, and resources that teach emotional intelligence and regulation can empower individuals with practical strategies and insights. Integrating emotional intelligence into educational curricula equips individuals from a young age with the foundational skills needed to navigate the complexities of emotions and interpersonal interactions.

Developing emotional regulation skills is an ongoing process that requires patience, self-compassion, and a commitment to growth. Reflective practices, such as journaling or regular self-assessment, provide individuals with a means to track progress, identify patterns, and celebrate successes. The acknowledgment that emotional regulation is a skill set that evolves fosters a growth mindset—a belief in one's capacity to learn and refine these skills through intentional effort and practice.

In conclusion, developing emotional regulation skills is a transformative journey that unfolds across self- awareness, mindfulness, and intentional action. As individuals cultivate the ability to navigate the intricate landscape of their emotions with grace and intention, they foster a harmonious relationship with their inner world and contribute to creating environments that support well-being, resilience, and authentic living.

CHAPTER VII

Mindful Relationships

Navigating Conflict in Intimate Relationships

In the tapestry of intimate relationships, conflict emerges as an inevitable thread, weaving through the shared experiences of couples as they navigate the complexities of human connection. Conflict, far from being a harbinger of doom, presents an opportunity for growth, understanding, and deepening emotional bonds. This section explores the complex dynamics of conflict in close relationships, looking at the causes of discord, how it affects people individually and in relationships, and providing helpful advice on resolving disputes amicably while pursuing empathy, resilience, and mutual well- being.

Intimate relationship conflict frequently stems from the complex interaction between personal preferences, expectations, and changing requirements. There is a chance for conflict when two distinct people come together, each bringing their background, morals, and communication preferences. Unfulfilled expectations, unsolved difficulties from the past, and the ups and downs of personal development further compound conflict. The first step toward managing conflicts with greater complexity and empathy is acknowledging the various origins of conflict.

Conflict in close relationships has a significant negative effect on people's emotional and mental health as well as their general quality of life. Conflict is frequently accompanied by physiological arousal, tension, and emotional anguish, which has a knock-on effect beyond the original point of contention. People may experience emotions such as hurt, disappointment, or irritation, and the relationship's emotional bond and sense of security may be undermined over time by unsolved issues. It is crucial to handle arguments tactfully while considering the personal effects of conflict.

Beyond its impact on individuals, conflict forever stains the fabric of close relationships. Unresolved disputes have the potential to develop into a pattern of disengagement, which can erode trust by encouraging emotional detachment. On the other hand, disagreement can strengthen emotional ties, improve communication, and increase a relationship's overall resilience if handled positively. How partners handle conflicts, and their willingness to use conflict as a catalyst for growth determine how conflict affects their relationships.

The ability to communicate effectively is essential for handling conflict. Partners are encouraged to share their wants and feelings honestly and clearly without passing judgment or leveling accusations. Mutual respect and empathy are fostered by active listening, which is defined as sincere attention to detail and a sincere attempt to comprehend the viewpoint of the other person.

Mastering emotional regulation techniques enables people to control their feelings during disagreements, halting the worsening of unpleasant feelings. Self-awareness, mindfulness exercises, and the capacity to pause before acting all help regulate emotions and allow more deliberate and controlled reactions.

Developing empathy is having the ability to comprehend and feel what a partner is feeling. Perspective-taking helps people to see things from their partner's point of view during a quarrel, which promotes empathy and a deeper understanding. Acknowledging the subjective experiences that each partner brings to the relationship improves empathy and reduces antagonistic dynamics.

At its core, conflict resolution is the ability to communicate and come to mutually acceptable conclusions. Instead of competing, partners are urged to work together to achieve win-win solutions that respect each person's interests and preferences. To solve problems constructively, one must dissect the current situation, find common ground, and collaborate to generate solutions.

A key component of constructive conflict resolution is setting and upholding personal boundaries. People are urged to assertively convey their wants and express their preferences and sentiments without violating their partner's rights. Establishing a harmonious equilibrium between aggressiveness and willingness to compromise benefits a positive power dynamic in relationships.

Consulting a couples therapist or relationship counselor can be quite beneficial when dealing with particularly difficult or persistent disputes. They can also offer insightful advice. A neutral environment provided by professional help allows couples to examine underlying problems, enhance their communication styles, and acquire effective conflict resolution techniques.

When conflict is seen from the perspective of personal development and evolution, its place in close relationships is redefined. Couples can welcome conflict as a chance for improved communication, self-discovery, and their relationship's growth rather than viewing it as a danger. When handled carefully and intentionally, conflict can be resolved, and one gains a greater understanding of themselves and their spouse, strengthening their bond.

Maintaining a healthy conflict culture in close relationships requires constant work and a shared dedication to development. Partners can actively participate in the following activities to promote a constructive response to conflict. An open and honest communication pattern, outside of specific issues, enables couples to discuss their desires, feelings, and worries in a less stressful environment. Frequent check-ins help foster a proactive, continuing conversation that lessens the chance that unresolved problems will decay over time.

Having common principles and long-term objectives in agreement lays the groundwork for harmony when disagreements arise. When couples know their goals in common, it's easier to put the partnership above personal preferences when arguments occur. Mastering the abilities of self-awareness, self-regulation, empathy, and effective communication is a necessary step toward developing emotional intelligence, and engaging in activities or practices that improve emotional intelligence individually and collectively can help couples build a stronger foundation for handling conflict.

A mutual sense of strength and flexibility is enhanced when resilience-building strategies purposefully strengthen relationships. This could be overcoming obstacles as a group, rejoicing in victories as a unit, and seeing disagreements as chances for growth and cooperative problem-solving. A collaborative perspective is fostered by realizing that both partners contribute to the development and well-being of the relationship. In addition to actively seeking feedback from one another and actively engaging in personal development, partners should also view disagreements as chances for mutual understanding and improvement.

Conflict arises in the complicated terrain of intimate relationships not as a threat but as a standard and transformational feature of human connection. Effective communication, emotional intelligence, and a dedication to both parties' well-being are necessary for navigating conflict. Couples set off on a path toward a more robust, meaningful, and connected relationship when they welcome conflict as a chance for learning, growth, and strengthening their emotional ties.

The skill of handling conflict turns into a team effort that incorporates understanding and resilience into the complex web of close relationships.

Friendships and Anger Management

Friendships, those unique and cherished connections that transcend the bounds of familial and romantic relationships, are pivotal in shaping the human experience. Within the tapestry of these bonds, joyous and challenging emotions weave a narrative that reflects the depth and resilience of these connections. Anger is one of the many emotions that might surface, but it's a particularly potent emotion that, if handled well, can strengthen bonds between people and promote personal development. This section explores the complex ties that exist between friendships and controlling anger. It looks at the causes of anger, how it affects relationships, and how to encourage constructive ways to express anger while maintaining strong bonds with friends.

The complicated and multidimensional emotion of anger frequently develops in reaction to injustices, perceived threats, or frustrations. Anger in the friendship setting can be brought on by various things, such as expectations that aren't realized, feelings of betrayal, or opposing moral principles. Anger in friendships can also stem from personal fears, traumatic events, or power and control issues in the relationship. Understanding the various causes of anger in friendships creates the foundation for a more complex and compassionate method of expressing and resolving it.

Anger has a significant negative effect on friendships, changing the emotional tone, the sense of trust, and the dynamics of the partnership as a whole. Unresolved rage can split people apart, causing emotional rifts and weakening the trust cornerstone of deep alliances. On the other hand, when handled positively, rage can act as a growth-promoting agent, encouraging candid conversations, firm boundaries, and a greater comprehension of one another's needs and viewpoints.

Anger's effects on friendships depend, in large part, on the techniques friends use to deal with and express their anger, as well as their shared will to seize these times to deepen their relationship.

Open Communication: Having open communication is essential to handling resentment in friendships. Friends are urged to be honest and vulnerable in sharing their ideas, emotions, and worries to foster genuine communication. Empathy is developed, and the emotional bond is strengthened by active listening, defined as a sincere attempt to comprehend the friend's point of view.

Developing empathy is having the ability to comprehend and feel what a buddy is feeling. In times of rage, friends can learn to see things from each other's perspective by practicing perspective-taking, which promotes empathy and a better comprehension of the issues causing the dispute. Acknowledging the unique subjective experiences that each friend contributes to the friendship fosters empathy and reduces antagonistic interactions.
Managing anger in friendships requires setting and honoring appropriate limits. To promote a respectful environment, friends are urged to express their wants and expectations in plain and concise terms. Setting limits guarantees both parties feel heard and understood in the relationship and prevents problems from worsening. The ability to manage anger in friendships requires the ability to solve problems productively. Friends can investigate possible solutions, cooperatively pinpoint the underlying reasons for disputes, and cooperate to discover solutions that respect each party's needs and viewpoints. Anger-fueled periods become chances for learning and progress for both parties when constructive problem-solving is applied.

Timely resolution of anger is essential to avoiding the build-up of unsolved disputes. Friends are urged to chatter about things that make them angry rather than staying silent or avoiding certain situations for extended periods. A prompt resolution of disputes strengthens the friendship's emotional safety net and the notion that disagreements can be handled respectfully and carefully. Friends coping with rage can benefit from taking time for introspection. Self-awareness is facilitated by taking the time to comprehend one's own emotional reactions, triggers, and communication patterns. Friends can then impart their wisdom to one another, helping to develop a deeper comprehension of one another's vibrant landscapes.

Friends who validate one other's feelings, even rage, can foster a caring atmosphere. Recognizing that anger is a normal and appropriate reaction in specific circumstances de-stigmatizes the feeling and promotes candid discussion about its causes and effects. By encouraging one another to talk honestly about their emotions, including rage, friends can foster an environment where emotional expression is valued in their relationships. Establishing an environment where both parties feel comfortable expressing their feelings promotes openness and vulnerability.

Adopting a mutual growth perspective in a friendship entails seeing disagreements and angry times as chances to grow and understand one another. Friends can address arguments with inquiry, looking for the root reasons and considering how the resolution process can help both parties develop. Friends can actively collaborate to develop emotional intelligence, a collection of abilities that includes effective communication, self-control, empathy, and self-awareness. Developing emotional intelligence improves one's capacity to control anger in a purposeful and considerate manner, which benefits friendship. Acknowledging and appreciating each friend's individuality—including their triggers and ways of expressing anger—helps to build acceptance in the friendship. Friends can handle disagreements by acknowledging the variety of viewpoints and fostering a conversation that respects the experiences and emotions of each party.

Managing anger in the context of friendships is a dynamic and ever-changing process that calls for empathy, intention, and a shared dedication to development. Friends can accept rage as a standard and healing part of human connection instead of seeing it as a danger to their friendship. Friends who deal with anger together in a genuine, vulnerable, and understanding manner go toward a deeper understanding, closer ties, and a connection that endures hardships with grace and resiliency. The skill of managing anger in friendships becomes a cooperative effort, incorporating knowledge and connection into the complex web of long-lasting and significant bonds.

Balancing Independence and Interdependence

Within the intricate tapestry of human connections, the delicate dance between independence and interdependence shapes the nature of relationships. The tension between autonomy and reliance, self-sufficiency and interconnectedness, defines the ebb and flow of dynamics in various spheres of life—romantic relationships, friendships, familial bonds, or the broader societal context. This section explores the complex interactions between interdependence and independence, looking at the reasons, obstacles, and solutions for striking a balance that promotes happy, lasting partnerships.

Independence and interdependence serve as fundamental dimensions along which relationships evolve and thrive. Pursuing personal objectives, independence, and self-reliance are essential to personal development and self-actualization. Conversely, interdependence stands for the mutual reliance and interconnectivity that characterize relationships. It entails cooperation, shared objectives, and a feeling of inclusion inside a more extensive relational framework. Building robust and long-lasting friendships requires finding the ideal balance between these two factors.

There are obstacles to striking a healthy balance between dependence and independence. People may struggle in relationships with control concerns, power dynamics, and the fear of losing their identity in the partnership. When opinions about what constitutes a "healthy" degree of independence or interdependence are shaped by cultural norms, personal histories, or societal expectations, finding a balance becomes much more difficult. To successfully navigate these obstacles, one must have a deep awareness of the particular dynamics of each relationship and be dedicated to creating an environment that supports the growth of both dimensions.

Establishing a balanced dynamic requires open and honest communication as a foundation. Friends, family, and partners must communicate their needs, expectations, and boundaries straightforwardly. This will help everyone understand how independence and interdependence behave in a relationship. Creating a safe environment for communication enables the negotiation of both individual and group requirements.

The key to balancing independence and reliance is cultivating an atmosphere that recognizes and respects individuality. Identity erosion can be avoided by acknowledging and respecting each person's distinct traits, objectives, and aspirations within the relationship. This respect for one another establishes the groundwork for a positive interdependence that values each person's independence.

Establishing a common framework based on shared values and objectives helps balance independence and interdependence. It is simpler to encourage one another's goals while preserving a sense of togetherness when people know the relationship's goals and ultimate objectives. Mutual values serve as tenets that guide the interdependence in the partnership.

Managing the tension between independence and interdependence requires setting and upholding boundaries. Having well-defined limits protects individuality and personal space while creating a feeling of security in the partnership. Setting sound boundaries promotes equilibrium so people or partners can prosper alone and together.

In partnerships, trust acts as a stabilizing factor, enabling a healthy balance between dependence and independence. Establishing trust in a relationship requires being open, dependable, and having faith in the kindness of the other party. When there is a basis of trust, people feel free to follow their paths without worrying about the relationship's interdependence being compromised.

Navigating the challenges of independence and dependency requires the cultivation of emotional intelligence. People who are sensitive to both their own and other people's emotions can react to their partners' needs and goals with empathy. Deep awareness of the subtleties in a relationship is fostered by emotional intelligence, which creates a dynamic that is harmonious and supportive of both parties.

Being open to change as the demands and circumstances of the partnership change is necessary to balance independence and interdependence. Being flexible helps people deal with life's unavoidable changes and obstacles without sacrificing their fundamental principles or sense of individual liberty. Adapting to change as a necessary component of the relationship path helps to maintain a robust and dynamic equilibrium.

People can evaluate their wants, anxieties, and desires in the framework of independence and interdependence by regularly reflecting on themselves. It is easier to approach the dynamics of a relationship with more awareness and intentionality when one is aware of one's motives and possible areas for improvement. Self-reflection helps to maintain and improve the harmony between independence and connectivity.

Social and cultural norms significantly impact how independence and reliance interact. The different cultural perspectives on the relative importance of individual liberty and group peace influence the expectations people bring to their relationships. Societal constructions, gender norms, and dominant ideologies further shape the story of independence and interdependence. Establishing a balanced dynamic that aligns with the genuine needs and ideals of the people involved requires acknowledging and resisting these outside pressures.

For the sake of one's own and other people's well-being, independence and interdependence must coexist in a balanced way. People comfortable with their freedom in a relationship are more likely to feel fulfilled, progress as people, and be happy with their lives in general. Simultaneously, partnerships that exhibit a positive interdependence foster a support network that strengthens shared happiness, emotional fortitude, and a feeling of community. An atmosphere where people can flourish, as well as the relationship itself, is created by a balanced dynamic.

In partnerships, the dance between independence and interdependence is a complex and dynamic process that calls for deliberate effort, honest communication, and a thorough comprehension of shared and individual needs. People help create empowering and enriching relationships as they negotiate this delicate interaction. Weaving strands of autonomy and connection into the complex tapestry of human interactions, striking a balance between independence and interdependence becomes a collaborative undertaking. Through accepting this delicate dance, people and relationships discover adaptability, development, and a happy interaction that endures.

CHAPTER VIII

Stress Management Techniques

Mindful Approaches to Stress Reduction

Stress has become a pervasive companion in the hustle and bustle of modern life, where demands and responsibilities often seem unrelenting. The complexities of work, relationships, and the ever-evolving landscape of daily existence contribute to heightened tension for many individuals. As a result, there is a rising recognition of the significance of stress reduction. In this context, mindfulness stands out as a potent and transformational strategy. This section explores mindful ways to reduce stress by examining the causes of stress, mindfulness concepts, and valuable tactics that enable people to develop a more resilient and balanced relationship with the obstacles life throws at them.

Although stress is frequently seen as a normal reaction to difficult circumstances, it has profound physiological and psychological effects. Stress can take many forms, from the primitive "fight or flight" reaction in our evolutionary past to the contemporary complications of a fast-paced world. Many people suffer from chronic stress as a result of pressures at work, interpersonal difficulties, financial worries, and the constant stimulation of the digital era. Acknowledging the complex characteristics of stress is an essential initial measure in tackling its effects on psychological, emotional, and physiological health.

Fundamentally, mindfulness is a secular method of improving well-being rooted in long-standing contemplative traditions, especially those of Buddhism. The goal of mindfulness is to cultivate heightened awareness and presence in the present moment, free from judgment. Observing their thoughts, feelings, and sensations encourages people to develop acceptance and non-reactivity. By focusing on the here and now, mindfulness offers a haven from the never-ending flow of regrets from the past or worries about the future, as well as a break from the ongoing stresses that are a part of everyday life.

In mindful breathing exercises, the breath, our ever-present companion, becomes the focus point of attention. People anchor themselves in the here and now by observing their breaths. When stresses get too much for a person to handle, mindful breathing acts as an anchor, a place of safety. This practice's ease of use belies its powerful ability to lower tension and foster tranquility.

As part of a mindfulness exercise called the body scan, one might methodically move one's attention over various bodily areas while focusing on tension, discomfort, or sensations. By developing a mind-body connection, this practice enables people to let go of physical tension and create a more acute awareness of the physical manifestations of stress. Frequent body scan meditations help one become calmer and more concentrated.

Bringing mindfulness to the physical world, mindful walking entails paying attention to each stride, the feel of the earth beneath the feet, and the surroundings. By encouraging people to take a break from the automatic nature of daily activities, this practice provides a brief period of relaxation and renewal. The act of walking mindfully creates a link between contemplative practice and daily mobility.

Mindful eating encourages people to fully appreciate each bite in a society where fast and distracted meals are the norm. Observing food's hues, textures, and flavors and the feelings experienced during chewing and swallowing are all part of the discipline. People can cultivate a better relationship with food and lessen the stress that comes with mindless intake by raising awareness of the act of eating.

When writing is done with complete awareness, it becomes a conscious activity that serves as a means of self-expression. Journaling mindfully entails recording ideas, emotions, and experiences in the here and now without passing judgment. Through introspection, people can discover patterns of their thoughts and feelings, which helps them comprehend stressors and valuable coping mechanisms.

Loving-kindness meditation, rooted in the Buddhist tradition, focuses on developing compassion and kindness toward oneself and others. People who repeat positive affirmations, like "May I be happy, may I be healthy," radiate kindness and love. In addition to lessening self-critical thoughts, this exercise cultivates an optimistic outlook that serves as a stress-reduction mechanism.

Being attentive to one's interactions with technology is essential in a time when digital gadgets rule the roost. A more conscious connection with screens involves being completely present when using technology, setting intentional boundaries, and undergoing digital detoxes. Utilizing technology mindfully reduces the stress of constant connectedness and information overload.

The scientific community has taken notice of mindfulness's ability to reduce stress despite its origins in contemplative traditions. According to neuroscientific research, regular mindfulness practice can alter the brain's structure, especially in areas related to attention, emotion management, and self-awareness. Studies using functional magnetic resonance imaging (fMRI) show changes in brain activity patterns, which may indicate that mindfulness benefits neural circuits related to stress reactions. The empirical data demonstrating mindfulness's effectiveness highlights the practice's potential as a valuable technique for stress management in the contemporary setting.

Dr. Jon Kabat-Zinn's evidence-based method, Mindfulness-Based Stress Reduction (MBSR), was created when mindfulness was incorporated into conventional therapy approaches. Yoga and mindfulness meditation are used in MBSR to help people develop a nonjudgmental awareness of the present moment. MBSR was initially created for those with chronic pain, but it has also shown promise in lowering stress and anxiety as well as improving general well-being. The organized program promotes long-term resilience in the face of stressors by giving participants valuable tools to incorporate mindfulness into their daily lives.

Cultivating a mindful lifestyle goes beyond specialized mindfulness exercises and entails bringing awareness to all facets of daily life. This entails going about daily tasks purposefully, like paying attention during talks, getting to chores, and finding beauty amid a hectic day. A mindful lifestyle is about consistently weaving awareness into one's life to build a stress-reduction and resilience reserve.

Mindfulness and resilience—the ability to overcome adversity—are closely related. Those who practice non-reactive awareness of their thoughts and feelings can better handle stressful situations calmly. Acceptance and an emphasis on the present moment are two aspects of mindfulness that help cultivate a mindset that sees setbacks as chances for development rather than insurmountable hurdles. This change in viewpoint strengthens psychological resilience and makes it easier for people to deal with life's inevitable ups and downs.

Since businesses realize that mindfulness can lower stress at work and improve employee well-being, the practice has become more prevalent in professional contexts. Workplace mindfulness programs typically involve mindfulness-based courses, guided meditation sessions, and campaigns to encourage a more mindful work environment. Organizations help create a more positive and productive work environment by giving employees the resources they need to manage stress and cultivate a stronger feeling of presence.

Although mindfulness originated in ancient contemplative traditions, it has since spread beyond national and cultural barriers. In the West, mindfulness has entered various domains, such as psychology, medicine, education, and business environments, and has become a secular practice. The widespread acceptance of mindfulness as a universal strategy for enhancing mental health and well-being is reflected in its global spread. Even with its significant effects and broad acceptance, mindfulness has its detractors. Some people can find it challenging to maintain a regular mindfulness practice because of time constraints, misgivings, or false beliefs about its intent. According to critics, the monetization of mindfulness, especially in the business sector, runs the risk of lessening its transformative power. Concerns have also been expressed regarding the appropriation of mindfulness from its spiritual and cultural roots.

Mindfulness stands out as a ray of resilience in the face of life's numerous stressors, providing a revolutionary method of stress reduction. Those who can anchor their attention to the present moment with acceptance and openness are better able to handle the challenges of everyday life. Individuals can develop a resilient and balanced relationship with stress by utilizing the practical tools outlined in the mindful approaches, including body scan meditations, breath awareness, and a conscious lifestyle. The ancient knowledge of present-moment awareness endures as a beacon of hope for cultivating well-being in the face of life's ups and downs as the science of mindfulness expands and its uses broaden. Mindfulness weaves threads of awareness, resilience, and a deep connection to the richness of the present moment into the fabric of stress reduction.

Incorporating Relaxation Exercises into Daily Life

In the relentless pace of modern life, where the demands of work, relationships, and personal responsibilities often seem ceaseless, the quest for tranquility becomes paramount. Amidst the din of daily stressors, the incorporation of relaxation exercises emerges as a transformative pathway toward reclaiming moments of calm and fostering well-being. This section aims to examine the art of integrating relaxation exercises into daily life. It will cover the importance of relaxation, various relaxation techniques, and valuable tips for blending peaceful moments into everyday living.

In summary, relaxation is a luxury and a vital aspect of overall health and well-being. Beyond the momentary comfort, relaxing has profound physiological and psychological advantages ingrained in the complex relationship between the mind and body. If chronic stress is not managed, it can lead to several health concerns, such as immune system damage, heart problems, and mental health disorders. Relaxation, conversely, acts as a counterbalance, promoting an equilibrium that enables people to face life's obstacles with fortitude, clarity, and a deep sense of peace.

The field of relaxation includes many methods, each providing a unique gateway into a peaceful haven. The variety of relaxation approaches, ranging from age-old customs to modern techniques, enables people to customize their strategy to their lifestyle, personal tastes, and the constantly changing nature of everyday obstacles.

Several relaxation techniques are based on the basic principle of breathing. Diaphragmatic and belly breathing are two examples of deep breathing techniques that operate as pillars to ground people in the present. People who intentionally control their breathing can release stress and foster a sense of peace by triggering the body's relaxation response.

Progressive Muscle Relaxation is a technique that comes from therapeutic interventions. It entails methodically tensing and then relaxing various muscle groups. This exercise helps relieve physical tension and increase awareness of one's own body sensations. By bridging the gap between the mental and physical domains, PMR provides a complete relaxing experience.

People can use their imaginations to enter peaceful mental landscapes through guided imagery and visualization. Through visualization exercises or guided imagery, people can induce relaxation that extends beyond the immediate stressors of their daily lives. This method uses the mutually beneficial interaction between emotional health and mental imagery.

With its roots in antiquated contemplative practices, mindfulness meditation has become well-known for its ability to ease tension and encourage relaxation. Practicing nonjudgmental awareness of the present moment teaches people to observe their thoughts and feelings without getting caught up in them. A calm and focused state of mind can be reached through mindfulness meditation.

Exercises like yoga and tai chi, which combine movement and awareness, provide a comprehensive approach to relaxing. The intentional and fluid motions and concentrated breathing awareness produce a harmonic fusion of the mental and physical realms. These age-old techniques foster a calm mental state and increase strength and flexibility.

Autogenic training, created in the early 20th century, consists of self-directed exercises meant to encourage mental and physical relaxation. People can learn to control their autonomic nervous system by repeatedly repeating mantras and visualizations that promote calmness. With autogenic training, people can trigger a relaxing response whenever they want.

Aromatherapy uses essential oils to create a sensory experience that enhances relaxation by utilizing the power of scent. Certain scents, like lavender, chamomile, or bergamot, have been demonstrated to have calming effects on the nervous system and can be added to an atmosphere that promotes relaxation, whether through diffusers, massage oils, or scented candles.

Spending time in nature is a powerful way to de-stress and provides a break from the bustle of the city. Spending time in a garden, going on nature walks, or just staring up at the sky can all help one feel refreshed by the sights, sounds, and rhythms of the natural world.

Although it is clear that relaxation techniques are appealing, the difficulty is in incorporating them into daily living in a smooth and effective way. It takes a combination of intention, inventiveness, and adaptability to master the art of relaxing. Empirical methods can enable people to include peaceful times into their daily lives without adding to the stress of an already busy day.

Acknowledging the notion of micro-retreats entails securing fleeting moments of relaxation within the constraints of a hectic routine. These mini-retreats, which can be as simple as a five-minute deep breathing practice at the office, a mindful walk during a break, or a brief period of guided imagery before bed, can become powerful sources of calm among the ups and downs of daily responsibilities.

In the same way people plan their meetings, appointments, and chores, setting aside time for leisure also conveys the value of well-being. Whether it's scheduling mindfulness meditation, yoga, or your go-to relaxation method for a certain amount of time every day, planning these sessions makes them more critical and guarantees that they happen.

Relaxation chances arise naturally when transitional situations are infused with mindfulness. A seamless shift in mental states can be facilitated by taking thoughtful breaths, doing a fast body scan, or practicing progressive muscle relaxation before bed, whether you're going from work to home, between chores, or before bed.

Recognizing the ubiquitous nature of technology in modern life, raising awareness of its use becomes essential. By establishing tech-free zones or designated times for digital detoxes, people can recover calm moments and lessen the overstimulation that can exacerbate stress.

Using current interests or pastimes as avenues for unwinding offers a smooth transition into everyday life. It's more sustainable to link relaxation with joyful activities, whether deep breathing exercises as a favorite activity, gardening with mindfulness, or walking as a moving meditation. Rearranging the physical space with intention can help create a relaxing atmosphere. The physical surroundings influence how the mind and emotions feel, whether through soothing hues, gentle lighting, or well-placed objects that promote peace.

Acknowledging the social aspect of leisure, partaking in peaceful pursuits alongside others cultivates a mutual feeling of well-being. The social element improves the relaxing experience, whether taking a yoga session with friends, deep breathing exercises, or just spending time in nature. When one approaches eating with mindfulness, it becomes a chance to unwind. A calm and conscious relationship with food is facilitated by savoring every bite, practicing gratitude for the sustenance, and being present throughout meals.

Attitudes toward well-being are shaped by cultural perceptions, which in turn affect how much relaxation is incorporated into daily life. Diverse cultural perspectives on leisure differ widely, frequently from customs, festivals, and group activities. Comprehending and accepting varied cultural viewpoints enhances relaxation, providing an expanded range of methods and perspectives on the shared human desire for peace of mind. There are numerous advantages to practicing relaxation techniques daily that go beyond just reducing stress.

Stress reduction is the primary and most direct advantage of relaxation techniques. Inducing the relaxation response, people can lessen the adverse physiological and psychological impacts of long-term stress, leading to a more composed and peaceful state of mind. Relaxation techniques have a calming influence on sleep as well. Regular practice lowers anxiety, increases relaxation, and creates a favorable physical and mental environment for rest. All of these factors lead to better sleep quality.

Relaxation methods help people become clearer mentally by reducing mental noise and encouraging present-moment awareness. Brain clarity improves problem-solving skills, cognitive function, and general productivity. There is a strong link between emotional health and relaxation. Relaxation techniques support emotional resilience, self-awareness, and a stable emotional state by facilitating the processing of emotions.

Relaxation techniques have a positive effect on physical health in addition to mental and emotional well-being. Regular relaxation is linked to various health benefits, such as lowered blood pressure, enhanced immunological function, reduced muscle tension, and overall well-being. Through the development of calm and collected thinking, relaxation exercises foster resilience. People who make relaxing a priority in their lives become better at handling stress and overcoming hardship. Exercises that promote relaxation affect the autonomic nervous system, bringing the parasympathetic (rest and digest) and sympathetic (fight-or-flight) branches into balance. This balance influences the general physiological equilibrium and resilience.

Despite the apparent advantages of relaxation techniques, people frequently face difficulties and obstacles while trying to stick to a regular schedule. Common barriers include time restraints, skepticism, perceived ineffectiveness, and trouble forming new habits. Recognizing the long-term advantages of regular relaxation and a tailored, step-by-step strategy is necessary to overcome these obstacles.

Incorporating relaxation techniques into everyday life is a transformational and approachable route in the quest for well-being. Whether it's via the movement of yoga, the simplicity of deep breathing, or the sensory experience of aromatherapy, people can recover peaceful moments from the chaos of contemporary life. The secret to successfully integrating relaxing is to deliberately weave serenity into everyday activities rather than relying solely on the grandeur of complex rituals. When people learn to value downtime, experiment with different approaches, and apply valuable tactics, they add calmness to their life's fabric. Relaxation transforms from a practice into a way of life—a deliberate and mindful way of living that fosters resilience, well-being, and a deep sense of inner peace.

Creating a Supportive Lifestyle

In the intricate dance of life, where demands, challenges, and the pursuit of personal growth intertwine, a supportive lifestyle emerges as a cornerstone for holistic well-being. A supportive lifestyle transcends adherence to specific practices; it embodies a comprehensive and intentional approach to nurturing physical, mental, and emotional health. This section explores developing a supporting lifestyle by reviewing the fundamental ideas, various elements, and practical tactics that enable people to build a robust and fulfilling life.

Fundamental values form the basis of a supporting lifestyle and act as beacons of guidance for anyone looking for a comprehensive approach to health and well-being. These values promote resilience, balance, and a sense of purpose and are the cornerstone of a supportive existence. The first step toward living a supportive lifestyle is becoming deeply aware of one's values, goals, strengths, and areas that require improvement. By developing self-awareness, people can make lifestyle decisions that are true to who they are, which leads to a sense of contentment and purpose.

A supportive lifestyle revolves around finding a careful balance between all aspects of life, including work, relationships, leisure, and personal growth. To achieve harmony, one must acknowledge how these components are interrelated and develop a routine that upholds balance and keeps well-being from eroding. One of the most essential characteristics of a supportive lifestyle is resilience, or the ability to adjust and overcome hardship. Resilience is the ability to deal with life's inevitable ups and downs by learning coping strategies, having an optimistic view, and embracing setbacks as opportunities for progress. Practicing mindfulness regularly acts as a foundation for a supportive way of living. Individuals can build a full and meaningful life experience, free from the constraints of past regrets or future fears, by practicing mindful awareness of the present moment.

A supportive lifestyle is made up of many different elements that work together to promote general well-being. These elements focus on various facets of life and promote a well-rounded approach to happiness and health. Making physical health a priority includes getting enough sleep, eating a nutritious and balanced diet, exercising frequently, and using preventative healthcare procedures. A supportive lifestyle is based on physical well-being, which lays the groundwork for emotional and mental fortitude.

Emotional and mental health are essential in a supporting lifestyle. Techniques like dynamic control, stress management, and mindfulness facilitate mental clarity, emotional resilience, and an optimistic outlook. Building supportive and meaningful relationships is essential to living a fulfilling life. Building solid relationships with friends, family, and the larger community creates a support system promoting emotional health and identity. A supportive way of living values lifelong learning and personal development. A sense of purpose and fulfillment can be attained by pursuing hobbies and passions, making significant goals, and partaking in mentally stimulating activities. Maintaining a supportive lifestyle requires striking a balance between personal and professional obligations. Ensuring that one's employment is in line with personal beliefs and permits significant involvement in other areas of life is known as work-life integration, and it improves one's general state of well-being.

For renewal and relaxation, leisure and recreational activities must be incorporated into daily life. Playtime, hobbies, and artistic endeavors add to a happy and well-rounded living. A supportive lifestyle includes environmental conservation in addition to personal well-being. Lifestyle choices that are eco-conscious, living sustainably, and connecting to the natural world all help foster a sense of interconnection and responsibility.

A supportive lifestyle frequently includes investigating and nourishing one's spiritual side. Spiritual well-being offers comfort and purpose via contemplative activities, meditation, or religious traditions. Creating a supportive lifestyle requires deliberate and doable tactics that complement the many elements and guiding concepts. These techniques allow people to create healthy habits, make thoughtful decisions, and develop environments promoting well-being.

Establishing attainable and significant objectives provides a road map for a helping lifestyle. A purposeful and intentional style of living is facilitated by the direction, drive, and sense of accomplishment that comes from having goals. Setting priorities for tasks that fit one's values and objectives is crucial to time management. Establishing a routine that balances work, play, relationships, and self-care helps people avoid burnout and leads to a positive way of life.

Positive routines must be incorporated into daily life to cultivate good habits. These habits improve general well-being, whether they involve stress-reduction techniques, mindful eating, regular exercise, or enough sleep. Establishing and upholding limits is essential to living a supportive lifestyle. Limiting job hours, social engagements, and other responsibilities helps people avoid burnout and retain their time.

When making decisions, people practicing mindfulness consider how those decisions affect their well-being and values. Making thoughtful decisions entails considering how decisions could affect different facets of life. Making self-care a priority entails deliberate actions that promote mental, emotional, and physical well-being. Self-care rituals, such as taking time for quiet introspection, engaging in revitalizing activities, or getting professional help when necessary, are essential to leading a supportive lifestyle.

Developing relationships within a community is one way to lead a supportive lifestyle. Volunteering, participating in group projects, and socializing all help create a feeling of community and purpose. People who regularly reflect on their lives can better evaluate how well their lifestyle fits their values and objectives. Reflection guarantees continuous alignment with a helpful way of living and acts as a checkpoint for improvements.

Attitudes toward well-being are shaped by cultural viewpoints, which in turn affect the idea of a supporting lifestyle. Diverse cultural perspectives on work, relationships, health, and leisure lead to various expressions of a supportive way of life. Understanding and valuing cultural variety broadens our perspective on what makes for a fulfilling and encouraging life.

Despite the advantages, people frequently encounter difficulties and obstacles when attempting to live a supportive lifestyle. Social factors, time restraints, outside expectations, and deeply set behaviors are typical roadblocks. It takes a combination of self-awareness, dedication, and a systematic approach to implementing supporting behaviors to overcome these obstacles.

The art of designing a supporting lifestyle appears as a significant and transformational undertaking in the fabric of human existence. A supportive lifestyle is more than just routines and habits; it is an intentional and purposeful way of living that fosters the complex relationships between mental clarity, emotional resilience, physical health, and a deep sense of purpose in life. People weave resilience, balance, and well-being into the fabric of their lives as they set out on this path. A supporting lifestyle becomes a guiding rhythm in the daily dance of life, balancing the various aspects and cultivating a vivid and flourishing way of being.

CHAPTER IX

Maintaining Mindful Masculinity

Integrating Mindful Practices into Daily Routine

In the fast-paced rhythm of modern life, where constant demands and distractions abound, incorporating mindful practices into the daily routine emerges as a transformative approach to fostering holistic well-being. Mindfulness, rooted in ancient contemplative traditions, is a practice that involves bringing focused attention to the present moment with an attitude of openness and non-judgment. This section explores the art of integrating mindful practices into daily life, delving into the profound impact of mindfulness on physical, mental, and emotional well-being. From the foundational principles that underpin mindfulness to practical strategies for seamlessly infusing mindfulness into routine activities, this exploration illuminates the transformative potential of cultivating presence in the tapestry of everyday existence.

At the core of mindfulness lie foundational principles that distinguish it as a unique and powerful practice. These principles provide the framework for cultivating a mindful approach to life, fostering a deep connection to the present moment and its richness. Mindfulness is grounded in the cultivation of present-moment awareness. It involves intentionally directing attention to the unfolding experience without being entangled in past regrets or future anxieties. Present-moment awareness is a gateway to a heightened sense of clarity and engagement with the nuances of daily life.

A fundamental tenet of mindfulness is approaching experiences with non-judgmental awareness. This involves observing thoughts, emotions, and sensations without labeling them good or bad. Non-judgmental awareness fosters a compassionate and accepting attitude toward oneself and the ever-changing landscape of the mind. Mindfulness acknowledges the impermanence of all things. Whether it's the fleeting nature of thoughts, the transient quality of emotions, or the impermanence of external circumstances, the practice encourages an acceptance of life's inherent ebb and flow. The breath serves as a foundational anchor in mindfulness practices. Individuals ground themselves in the present moment by directing attention to the sensations of breathing. The breath becomes a constant companion, a source of stability amidst the dynamic nature of thoughts and emotions.

While the principles of mindfulness provide a philosophical foundation, integrating mindful practices into daily life requires practical strategies that align with the realities of a busy and dynamic routine. These strategies empower individuals to infuse moments of mindfulness into various activities, fostering a continuous and accessible cultivation of presence. Commencing the day with a mindful morning routine establishes a positive and centered foundation. This may involve conscious breathing while brushing teeth, savoring the flavors of breakfast, or taking a moment of quiet reflection before the day unfolds. A mindful start sets the tone for a more intentional and present day.

Incorporating short, mindful breathing breaks throughout the day is a potent strategy for cultivating presence. Whether it's a few conscious breaths before entering a meeting, waiting in line, or transitioning between tasks, these breaks create islands of calm within the hustle of daily life. Transforming meals into mindful experiences involves savoring each bite, appreciating the textures and flavors, and being fully present while eating. Mindful eating enhances the enjoyment of food and fosters a healthier relationship with nourishment.

Routine activities such as walking can become opportunities for mindfulness. By bringing awareness to each step, the sensation of movement, and the surrounding environment, individuals can infuse a sense of mindfulness into walking. This practice extends the benefits of mindfulness to physical well-being. Recognizing the pervasive role of technology, integrating mindfulness into digital interactions becomes crucial. This involves setting intentional boundaries for screen time, practicing mindful technology use, and taking digital detox breaks to prevent overstimulation and promote presence.
Commuting, often considered a mundane necessity, can be transformed into a mindful practice. Whether driving, walking, or using public transportation, individuals can bring awareness to the sensations of movement, the environment, and the act of commuting, turning a routine activity into a mindful journey. Infusing mindfulness into work involves approaching tasks with focused attention, taking short mindfulness breaks between assignments, and cultivating a non-judgmental awareness of the work environment. Mindful work practices increase productivity, creativity, and overall job satisfaction. Wrapping up the day with a conscious evening reflection allows individuals to review the day's experiences with a non-judgmental awareness. This may involve journaling, a brief meditation, or taking moments to acknowledge the day's joys and challenges openly.

Exploring real-life examples of individuals who have successfully integrated mindfulness into their daily routines provides inspiration and insights into the transformative power of this practice. Case studies and success stories showcase how mindfulness can positively impact mental health, enhance resilience, and contribute to a more fulfilling and present way of life. Parents who incorporate mindfulness into their parenting practices report increased patience, improved communication with their children, and a greater capacity to handle the challenges of raising a family. Mindful parenting involves being fully present during interactions with children, cultivating non-reactive responses, and fostering a deep connection with the joys of parenthood.

Organizations that introduce mindfulness programs witness positive shifts in workplace culture. Employees who engage in mindfulness practices report reduced stress, increased focus, and enhanced collaboration. Mindfulness in the workplace includes activities such as guided meditations, mindfulness workshops, and initiatives that promote a more present and compassionate work environment. Leaders who embrace mindfulness exhibit emotional intelligence, resilience, and the ability to make thoughtful decisions. Mindful leadership involves intentionally leading, actively listening to team members, and creating a work environment that values productivity and well-being.

Integrating mindful practices into daily life yields myriad benefits that extend across physical, mental, and emotional dimensions. These benefits contribute to a more resilient, centered, and fulfilling lifestyle. One of the primary benefits of mindfulness is its profound impact on stress reduction. By cultivating present-moment awareness and non-judgmental acceptance, individuals can navigate stressors with greater ease, preventing the accumulation of chronic stress.

Mindfulness enhances cognitive abilities by promoting focused attention. Regular practice sharpens the ability to concentrate on tasks, make clear decisions, and engage in activities with heightened awareness. Mindfulness equips individuals with tools for emotional regulation. By observing emotions with non-judgmental awareness, individuals can respond to situations with greater emotional intelligence, preventing impulsive reactions and fostering a balanced emotional state.

The practice of mindfulness has been linked to improved sleep quality. By calming the mind and reducing rumination, individuals who engage in mindfulness find it easier to relax and achieve restful sleep. Mindfulness deepens self-awareness by bringing attention to thoughts, emotions, and bodily sensations. This heightened awareness facilitates a better understanding of oneself, leading to personal growth and a more authentic way of living.

Mindful practices foster a stronger mind-body connection, especially those involving breath awareness and movement. This connection contributes to overall physical well-being and harmony between the mental and physical dimensions. Mindfulness nurtures resilience by instilling a mindset that views challenges as opportunities for growth. Individuals who practice mindfulness develop a capacity to bounce back from adversity, adapt to change, and face life's uncertainties with equanimity. The cultivation of present-moment awareness and non-judgmental acceptance extends to interpersonal relationships. Mindful individuals exhibit enhanced communication skills, empathy, and a capacity to connect with others on a deeper level.
While the benefits of mindfulness are evident, individuals may encounter challenges and barriers in integrating mindful practices into their daily routines. Common obstacles include time constraints, skepticism, difficulty establishing a consistent practice, and misconceptions about the nature of mindfulness. Overcoming these challenges requires a patient and gradual approach, coupled with an understanding of mindfulness practice's flexible and adaptable nature.

In the symphony of modern existence, the integration of mindful practices into daily routines emerges as a harmonious melody—a transformative journey toward holistic well-being. From the foundational principles that ground mindfulness to the practical strategies that infuse presence into routine activities, individuals embark on a path that transcends the boundaries of time and circumstance. Mindfulness, when woven into the fabric of daily life, becomes a way of being—a conscious and intentional approach that nurtures the intricate connections between mind, body, and spirit. As individuals engage in the art of cultivating presence, they discover the profound impact of mindfulness on stress reduction, focus, emotional regulation, and overall resilience. In the dance of daily existence, mindfulness becomes a guiding rhythm—an invitation to savor the richness of each moment and embrace life with a heightened sense of clarity and appreciation.

Recognizing Progress and Celebrating Success

In pursuing personal growth and achievement, the journey is often marked by milestones—small victories, significant accomplishments, and moments of triumph that collectively contribute to the tapestry of an individual's life. However, individuals may overlook the importance of recognizing progress and celebrating success amidst the ceaseless pursuit of goals. This section delves into the significance of acknowledging milestones and exploring this practice's psychological, emotional, and motivational impact. From understanding the dynamics of progress recognition to the diverse ways success can be celebrated, this exploration sheds light on the transformative power of fostering a culture of appreciation and reflection in the ongoing narrative of personal development.

At its core, progress recognition taps into the fundamental principles of positive psychology—a field that focuses on understanding and enhancing well-being. Recognizing and acknowledging progress catalyzes cultivating a positive mindset and fostering intrinsic motivation. Understanding the psychological dynamics behind progress recognition unveils its role in shaping attitudes, reinforcing positive behaviors, and contributing to an individual's overall sense of fulfillment.

The concept of positive reinforcement, a fundamental principle in behavioral psychology, underscores the importance of acknowledging and rewarding positive behaviors. When individuals receive recognition for their efforts and achievements, it reinforces the connection between their actions and positive outcomes, encouraging the repetition of these behaviors. Intrinsic motivation, the internal drive that propels individuals to engage in activities for their inherent enjoyment or personal satisfaction, is closely linked to progress recognition. When individuals perceive that their efforts are acknowledged and appreciated, it enhances their sense of competence and autonomy, fueling intrinsic motivation to continue their pursuit of goals.

Progress recognition is pivotal in developing self-efficacy—the belief in one's ability to accomplish tasks and achieve goals. Regular acknowledgment of progress reinforces individuals' confidence in their capabilities, empowering them to tackle challenges with a heightened sense of self-assurance. Recognizing progress creates a positive feedback loop—a continuous cycle of setting goals, making progress, receiving recognition, and being motivated to set new goals. This cyclical process contributes to an upward spiral of growth, resilience, and an optimistic outlook on future challenges.

They celebrated success, big or small, as essential to personal growth and well-being. The celebration goes beyond mere acknowledgment; it involves consciously taking the time to commemorate achievements, fostering a sense of joy, gratitude, and a deeper connection to one's journey of self-discovery. Celebrating success evokes positive emotions, creating a reservoir of positive experiences that individuals can draw upon during challenging times. The emotional resonance of success celebrations contributes to a more resilient and emotionally balanced mindset.

Celebrations provide an opportunity for reflection and gratitude. Taking a moment to appreciate the progress made, the lessons learned, and the support received enhances individuals' awareness of the richness of their experiences, fostering a deeper connection to the journey. Celebrating success serves as a powerful motivator for future endeavors. The sense of accomplishment and the joy derived from celebrating success create an internal motivation that propels individuals forward, instilling confidence and a belief in their ability to overcome future challenges. The act of celebration contributes to the creation of a positive narrative about one's journey. By intentionally marking successes, individuals shape a narrative that emphasizes resilience, growth, and the ability to overcome obstacles—a narrative that becomes a source of inspiration and empowerment.

Recognizing progress can take various forms, adapting to individual preferences, goals, and the nature of the achievements. The diversity of recognition methods ensures that individuals can find approaches that resonate with them and align with their unique personal development journey. The practice of acknowledging personal progress begins with self-awareness and self-acknowledgment. Individuals can consciously reflect on their achievements, no matter how small, and recognize the effort invested in their pursuits.

Keeping a progress journal allows individuals to document their journey, record milestones, and overcome challenges. Reading through the journal provides a tangible representation of progress, serving as a reminder of the resilience and growth experienced along the way. Establishing clear and achievable goals provides a roadmap for progress. Regularly reviewing and adjusting these goals allows individuals to track their advancement, celebrate the milestones achieved, and recalibrate their trajectory for continued growth.

Sharing achievements with trusted friends, family members, or mentors allows for peer recognition. The validation and encouragement from others contribute to a sense of community and support, reinforcing the importance of the achieved milestones. Visualization involves mentally rehearsing and envisioning successful outcomes. Incorporating visualization techniques allows individuals to cultivate a positive mindset, making progress tangible in the mind's eye and creating a sense of achievement. Implementing personal reward systems provides a natural form of recognition. Individuals can establish rewards for reaching specific milestones, whether treating themselves to a favorite activity, indulging in a hobby, or enjoying a well-deserved break.

Celebrating success is a dynamic and personal experience, with individuals having the flexibility to choose methods that resonate with their values, preferences, and achievements. The diversity of celebration methods ensures individuals can craft meaningful and memorable experiences. A day or weekend for personal reflection and self-care is a powerful celebration. Whether it's a quiet retreat in nature, a spa day, or a period of intentional reflection, carving out time for self-celebration provides a space for rejuvenation and gratitude.

Symbolic acts, such as lighting a candle, releasing a balloon, or creating a piece of art, can serve as tangible representations of success. These acts carry personal significance, acting as symbols of accomplishment and growth. Celebrating success with friends, family, or colleagues enhances the joy of achievement. Hosting a gathering, sharing a meal, or organizing a small event allows individuals to bask in the support and camaraderie of those who have been part of their journey.

Expressing gratitude for the support received during the journey is a meaningful way to celebrate success. Whether through handwritten notes, heartfelt conversations, or a gratitude journal, acknowledging the contributions of others fosters a sense of connection and appreciation. Engaging in creative outlets, such as writing, painting, or crafting, provides a space for self- expression and celebration. Creating a tangible representation of success allows individuals to externalize their achievements and reflect on their journey uniquely. Viewing successes as opportunities for continued learning and growth reframes the celebration process. Individuals can celebrate by exploring new interests, taking a course, or delving into areas that align with their aspirations.

Cultural perspectives play a significant role in shaping attitudes toward recognition and celebration. Different cultures may have distinct rituals, traditions, and social norms that influence how individuals perceive and express acknowledgment of progress and celebration of success. Embracing and understanding diverse cultural perspectives enriches the collective tapestry of recognition practices.

Despite the benefits, individuals may encounter challenges and barriers to recognizing progress and celebrating success. Common obstacles include perfectionism, self-doubt, societal expectations, and the fear of appearing boastful. Overcoming these challenges requires a shift in mindset, self-compassion, and a commitment to valuing one's journey.

In the unfolding narrative of personal growth and achievement, recognizing progress and celebrating success emerge as vital threads that weave richness, resilience, and joy into an individual's journey. From the psychological underpinnings that highlight the transformative impact of acknowledgment to the diverse ways in which success can be celebrated, the exploration illuminates the profound significance of cultivating a culture of appreciation and reflection. As individuals embrace the habit of acknowledging milestones, they tap into the positive feedback loop of positive reinforcement, intrinsic motivation, and increased self-efficacy. Simultaneously, celebrating success becomes an art—a dynamic and personal expression that infuses joy, gratitude, and a deeper connection to the journey of self-discovery. In the collective celebration of achievements, individuals foster a positive mindset and contribute to a narrative that emphasizes resilience, growth, and the capacity to overcome obstacles. As the journey unfolds, recognizing progress and celebrating success become integral companions, guiding individuals toward a more fulfilling, balanced, and meaningful existence.

Continued Growth and Lifelong Learning

In the intricate dance of life, where time flows ceaselessly, and the landscape of experience evolves, the pursuit of continued growth and lifelong learning emerges as an enduring and transformative journey. Beyond the confines of formal education, the commitment to ongoing development becomes a guiding principle—a testament to the human capacity for adaptation, curiosity, and resilience. This section delves into the multifaceted dimensions of continued growth and lifelong learning, exploring the profound impact of these pursuits on personal development, professional fulfillment, and the broader fabric of society. From understanding the underlying principles that drive the desire for learning to explore diverse avenues through which individuals can foster ongoing growth, this exploration unravels the tapestry of a life dedicated to pursuing knowledge, wisdom, and the perpetual expansion of horizons.

At the heart of the human experience lies an inherent drive for learning—a primal curiosity that propels individuals to explore, understand, and make sense of the world around them. From the early stages of childhood to the twilight years of life, the quest for knowledge remains a dynamic force, reflecting the fundamental nature of human cognition and the insatiable desire to comprehend the intricacies of existence.

Cognitive curiosity, the innate inclination to seek out new information and experiences, is a driving force for continued growth. This curiosity manifests early in life as children explore their surroundings, ask probing questions, and engage in playful learning. Throughout the lifespan, cognitive curiosity evolves, guiding individuals to seek intellectual stimulation and novelty. The pursuit of lifelong learning is intricately tied to adaptation and resilience. In a world characterized by rapid change and evolving challenges, individuals who embrace lifelong learning develop the adaptability and resilience to navigate uncertainties, acquire new skills, and thrive in dynamic environments.

Lifelong learning is a testament to the enduring nature of intellectual engagement. Whether through formal education, self-directed learning, or experiential discovery, individuals prioritizing ongoing intellectual stimulation cultivate a mindset that values continuous knowledge expansion and mastery in various domains.

Lifelong learning catalyzes multifaceted personal development, fostering growth across cognitive, emotional, and interpersonal dimensions. Committing to ongoing learning becomes a pathway to self-discovery, enhanced well-being, and a deeper understanding of one's unique place. Engaging in lifelong learning activities, such as reading, attending workshops, or pursuing educational courses, enriches cognitive abilities. Exposure to new ideas, perspectives, and information stimulates mental faculties, enhancing critical thinking, problem-solving skills, and the capacity for complex reasoning.

Lifelong learning contributes to the development of emotional intelligence—an essential aspect of personal growth. Individuals who actively seek to understand and manage their emotions, empathize with others, and navigate interpersonal dynamics are better equipped to build meaningful relationships and navigate life's challenges with emotional resilience. The dynamic nature of lifelong learning cultivates adaptability and flexibility. Individuals who embrace continuous growth develop a mindset that views challenges as opportunities for learning and adaptation. This adaptive resilience enables them to navigate change with optimism and a willingness to explore new possibilities. Lifelong learning fosters a culture of self-reflection and self-awareness. As individuals acquire new knowledge and skills, they develop a deeper understanding of their strengths, values, and areas for improvement. This heightened self-awareness becomes a foundation for intentional personal development.

Pursuing continued growth and lifelong learning

transcends personal development, extending its influence into professional fulfillment. In a rapidly evolving global landscape, individuals who prioritize ongoing learning enhance their career prospects and contribute to the resilience and innovation of the broader workforce. Lifelong learning is a gateway to skill development and mastery. In the professional sphere, acquiring new skills and staying abreast of industry trends is essential for career advancement. Individuals who invest in continuous learning position themselves as valuable contributors, capable of adapting to evolving job requirements.

Lifelong learning fosters career adaptability—the ability to

navigate and thrive in a changing professional landscape. As industries transform, individuals who cultivate a mindset of continuous growth exhibit the flexibility and resilience needed to transition between roles, industries, and career trajectories. Ongoing learning sparks innovation and creativity. Individuals exposed to diverse ideas, perspectives, and methodologies are likelier to think creatively and contribute to innovative solutions in their professional endeavors. Lifelong learners become catalysts for positive change and progress within their organizations. Lifelong learning often involves engagement with diverse communities, workshops, and networking opportunities. These interactions create avenues for professional networking, allowing individuals to connect with like-minded peers, mentors, and experts in their field. These networks become valuable resources for collaboration, mentorship, and career support.

The avenues for lifelong learning are as diverse as the interests and aspirations of individuals. From formal education to informal learning experiences, the landscape of lifelong learning encompasses a rich array of possibilities that cater to different preferences, lifestyles, and stages of life. Formal education, whether pursued through traditional academic institutions or online platforms, remains a cornerstone of lifelong learning. Individuals may enroll in degree programs, certifications, or short courses to deepen their knowledge in specific fields and acquire recognized credentials.

Self-directed learning empowers individuals to take control of their educational journey. Through self-guided exploration of books, online resources, and hands-on projects, individuals can pursue areas of personal interest, develop new skills, and expand their knowledge independently. The workplace serves as a dynamic learning environment. Employers increasingly recognize the value of investing in employee training and development programs, providing opportunities for skill enhancement, leadership training, and professional growth within one's job role.

The advent of online learning platforms has revolutionized the accessibility of educational resources. Platforms offering courses, webinars, and tutorials cater to diverse interests and allow individuals to learn at their own pace, often from the comfort of their homes. Community education programs offered by local organizations, libraries, and community centers provide accessible avenues for learning. These programs cover various topics and often involve hands-on workshops, discussion groups, and collaborative learning experiences. Membership in professional associations and conference attendance offer opportunities for specialized learning and networking within specific industries. These events provide exposure to cutting-edge developments, industry best practices, and the chance to connect with experts in the field.

While the benefits of lifelong learning are evident, individuals may encounter challenges and barriers on their journey. Common obstacles include time constraints, financial considerations, self-doubt, and resistance to change. Overcoming these challenges requires a proactive approach, resourcefulness, and a commitment to prioritizing personal and professional growth.

Cultural perspectives significantly influence attitudes toward lifelong learning. In some cultures, the pursuit of education is highly valued and ingrained in societal norms, while in others, cultural factors may pose barriers to embracing continuous learning. Recognizing and respecting diverse cultural perspectives on education is essential for fostering a global culture of lifelong learning.

In the tapestry of human existence, the commitment to continued growth and lifelong learning emerges as a thread that weaves through the fabric of personal development, professional fulfillment, and societal progress. From the inherent drive for learning that defines the human experience to the multifaceted dimensions of ongoing growth, individuals embark on a journey that transcends the boundaries of age, circumstance, and formal education. Lifelong learning becomes a dynamic force—a source of cognitive enrichment, emotional intelligence, and adaptability that shapes the trajectory of personal and professional endeavors.

As individuals embrace diverse avenues for learning, from formal education to self-directed exploration, they contribute to their development and the innovation and resilience of the broader societal tapestry. The challenges and barriers encountered along the way serve as opportunities for resilience and resourcefulness, highlighting the transformative power of a mindset dedicated to the perpetual expansion of horizons. In the ever-expanding quest for knowledge and wisdom, continued growth and lifelong learning become not only a personal pursuit but a collective endeavor—an affirmation of the human spirit's capacity for curiosity, adaptation, and an unwavering commitment to the pursuit of a life well-lived.

CONCLUSION

Encouragement for Ongoing Personal Development

In the grand tapestry of life, where the threads of experience weave a complex narrative, the journey of ongoing personal development emerges as a profound and transformative odyssey. Rooted in the belief that individuals possess an innate capacity for growth and self-improvement, ongoing personal development is a dynamic process that extends beyond formal education and professional endeavors. This section explores the vital role encouragement plays in fostering and sustaining the journey of personal development. From understanding the psychological foundations underpinning the desire for growth to exploring the diverse forms of encouragement that propel individuals forward, this exploration aims to illuminate the transformative power of supportive environments and the intrinsic motivation that drives individuals toward realizing their full potential.

At the core of ongoing personal development lies a profound psychological underpinning—the inherent human desire for growth, self-discovery, and the pursuit of a more fulfilled existence. Rooted in the following principles, the journey of personal development becomes a testament to the dynamism of the human spirit. The belief in innate human potential underscores the foundations of personal growth. Individuals harbor latent capacities for learning, adaptation, and acquiring new skills. Encouragement catalyzes unlocking and harnessing this innate potential, paving the way for continuous growth.

Drawing inspiration from Maslow's hierarchy of needs, ongoing personal development aligns with the pinnacle of self-actualization—a state in which individuals strive to realize their unique capabilities and fulfill their highest potential. Encouragement becomes a driving force in the journey toward self-actualization, propelling individuals to realize their aspirations. The intrinsic motivation to pursue personal development is a crucial psychological factor. Unlike external motivators, such as rewards or recognition, inherent motivation arises from an individual's desires and values. Encouragement nurtures this intrinsic motivation, serving as a supportive force that reinforces the pursuit of personal growth for its inherent rewards.

Encouragement is a cornerstone in personal development, providing the necessary nourishment for the seeds of potential to flourish. It transcends mere motivation and serves as a dynamic force that sustains individuals through challenges, instills confidence, and creates an environment conducive to continuous learning and growth. Encouragement builds confidence, fostering a belief in one's abilities and potential. When individuals receive positive reinforcement and acknowledgment for their efforts, it cultivates a sense of self-efficacy—the belief in one's capacity to achieve goals. This confidence becomes a driving force for tackling challenges and pursuing new opportunities.

The fear of failure often acts as a deterrent to personal development. Encouragement, however, transforms the narrative around failure. When individuals are supported and reassured that setbacks are a natural part of the learning process, it mitigates the fear of failure, allowing them to embrace challenges with resilience and a growth mindset. Encouragement creates supportive environments that nourish personal development. Whether in familial, educational, or professional settings, environments prioritizing positive reinforcement and constructive feedback foster a culture where individuals feel empowered to explore their potential without fear of judgment. Encouragement taps into intrinsic motivation—the internal drive that fuels ongoing personal development. When individuals receive encouragement, it reinforces their inner desires for growth and self-improvement, making pursuing personal development a source of intrinsic satisfaction rather than external validation.

Encouragement manifests in various forms, adapting to individuals' unique needs, preferences, and aspirations. Recognizing the diverse ways encouragement can be expressed enhances its impact, creating a nuanced and personalized approach to fostering ongoing personal development. Offering positive feedback is a fundamental form of encouragement. Acknowledging and affirming individuals for their achievements, progress, and efforts creates a positive feedback loop. This positive reinforcement is a powerful motivator, reinforcing the connection between actions and positive outcomes.

Contrary to its negative connotations, constructive criticism can be a form of encouragement when delivered with empathy and a focus on improvement. Providing thoughtful feedback that highlights areas for growth and offers guidance fosters a sense of support and a commitment to continuous improvement. Mentorship plays a pivotal role in encouraging personal development. Through their guidance, wisdom, and shared experiences, mentors provide individuals with valuable insights and perspectives. The mentor-mentee relationship is a source of inspiration and encouragement, facilitating the transfer of knowledge and skills.

Leading by example is a subtle yet powerful form of encouragement. Individuals who model behaviors aligned with ongoing personal development inspire others to embark on similar journeys. This modeling can involve demonstrating resilience in the face of challenges, embracing a growth mindset, and displaying a commitment to lifelong learning. Celebrating milestones, no matter how small, is a celebratory form of encouragement. Recognizing and commemorating personal, academic, or professional achievements creates a positive atmosphere that reinforces the importance of the ongoing journey of personal development.

Encouragement is a dynamic force that evolves to meet the changing needs of individuals across different life stages. From childhood to adulthood and into the later years of life, the role of encouragement adapts, providing continuous support and motivation for ongoing personal development. In childhood, encouragement is foundational to the development of a growth mindset. Positive reinforcement, praise for effort, and a supportive learning environment contribute to a child's confidence, curiosity, and enthusiasm for learning. Encouragement in education sets the stage for a lifelong love of learning.

During adolescence, encouragement becomes crucial in navigating identity formation and personal growth. Positive reinforcement for exploring interests, setting goals, and building resilience helps adolescents develop a sense of purpose and confidence in their evolving identities. In early adulthood, encouragement is pivotal in career development and pursuing personal aspirations. Supportive mentors, positive feedback in the workplace, and constructive guidance contribute to individuals' professional growth and confidence in their abilities. Individuals often encounter transitions and reflections on personal and professional accomplishments in midlife. Encouragement during this stage involves recognizing the value of accumulated experiences, supporting individuals as they reassess goals, and offering guidance as they navigate new opportunities for personal development. In later life, encouragement remains essential for promoting lifelong learning and pursuing new interests. Positive reinforcement for engaging in educational activities, acquiring new skills, and embracing novel experiences contributes to cognitive vitality and a sense of fulfillment.

While encouragement is a powerful catalyst for ongoing personal development, individuals may encounter challenges and barriers that impede support reception. Common obstacles include a lack of positive role models, societal expectations, self-doubt, and a reluctance to seek guidance. Overcoming these challenges requires a shift in mindset, a cultivation of resilience, and an awareness of the transformative impact of encouragement.

Cultural perspectives significantly influence the dynamics of encouragement. Different cultures may have distinct approaches to expressing support and motivation, and societal norms may shape how individuals perceive and respond to encouragement. Acknowledging and respecting diverse cultural perspectives on encouragement fosters a more inclusive and supportive environment for ongoing personal development.

In the symphony of human existence, encouragement emerges as a harmonious melody—a transformative force that nurtures the seeds of potential and propels individuals toward ongoing personal development. From the innate human desire for growth to the psychological foundations that underpin the journey of self- improvement, encouragement becomes a dynamic catalyst that sustains individuals through the challenges and triumphs of their unique odyssey. Through diverse forms such as positive feedback, mentorship, modeling behavior, and celebrating milestones, encouragement creates a supportive ecosystem that fosters confidence, resilience, and a commitment to continuous learning. As the tapestry of life unfolds across different stages, encouragement adapts, providing unwavering support from childhood through adolescence, early adulthood, midlife, and into the later years. Challenges and barriers may arise, but the transformative power of encouragement lies in its ability to transcend obstacles and inspire individuals to overcome self-doubt, societal expectations, and the fear of failure. Cultivating a culture of encouragement is not only a personal responsibility but a collective endeavor—an affirmation of the belief that every individual possesses the potential for ongoing personal development. In the spirit of encouragement, the journey becomes more than a solitary pursuit; it becomes a shared celebration of human resilience, growth, and the boundless possibilities that unfold when individuals are empowered to realize their full potential.

Resources for Further Support

Embarking on a personal development journey is a courageous and transformative endeavor but not a solitary pursuit. Recognizing the importance of seeking support and guidance is integral to navigating the complexities of self-discovery and growth. This section explores the diverse resources available to individuals seeking further support on their personal development journey. From professional assistance to community networks, self-help tools, and technological innovations, these resources form a rich tapestry that can provide encouragement, knowledge, and practical strategies for overcoming challenges and fostering ongoing personal development.

Therapy and Counseling: Mental health professionals, including therapists and counselors, offer valuable support in navigating personal challenges, managing stress, and addressing emotional well-being. Individuals can explore their thoughts and feelings through one-on-one sessions, gaining insights that contribute to personal growth. Life coaches specialize in guiding individuals toward achieving personal and professional goals. These professionals provide structured support, motivation, and strategic planning to help individuals overcome obstacles and positively change various aspects of their lives.

For those navigating career-related challenges, career counselors offer insights into aligning personal values with professional goals, making informed career decisions, and developing strategies for advancement. Different modalities of psychotherapy, such as cognitive-behavioral therapy (CBT), psychodynamic therapy, or mindfulness-based approaches, can be tailored to address specific needs. Psychotherapy helps individuals explore patterns of thinking and behavior, fostering self-awareness and promoting positive change. Personal development is intimately connected with physical well-being. Nutritional counselors can guide maintaining a healthy lifestyle, managing stress through nutrition, and fostering habits that contribute to overall well-being.

Many self-help books, personal development literature, and educational resources are available to those seeking knowledge and inspiration. Authors and thought leaders in the personal development space offer valuable insights and practical strategies for growth. Numerous online platforms provide courses and webinars on various personal development topics. These resources offer the flexibility to learn at one's own pace and explore specific areas of interest, from mindfulness and resilience to goal setting and time management.

Podcasts and audiobooks are accessible mediums for absorbing information on the go. Personal development podcasts feature interviews, discussions, and expert insights, while audiobooks provide a convenient way to engage with written content. Websites and blogs dedicated to personal development offer a wealth of articles, resources, and tools. These platforms cover diverse topics, providing information on self-discovery, emotional intelligence, and practical strategies for personal growth.

Whether online or in-person, joining support groups connects individuals with others who share similar experiences. Support groups provide a space for sharing challenges, receiving empathy, and gaining perspectives on personal development. Attending networking events in professional or community settings facilitates connections with like-minded individuals. These events offer opportunities for collaboration, mentorship, and the exchange of ideas.

Local community centers often host workshops, seminars, and events focused on personal development. Engaging with community organizations provides access to resources and support networks within one's geographical area. Online communities such as Facebook, LinkedIn, or specialized forums offer spaces for individuals to connect, share insights, and seek advice on personal development journeys.

Various apps focus on mental health and well-being, providing features such as guided meditation, mood tracking, and cognitive-behavioral exercises. These apps offer convenient tools for individuals to integrate into their daily lives. Platforms offering online therapy sessions connect individuals with licensed therapists through virtual sessions. This option provides flexibility and accessibility for those facing barriers to in-person therapy.

Apps dedicated to mindfulness and meditation guide individuals in developing a regular practice. These apps offer exercises, meditation sessions, and resources to enhance emotional well-being. Software applications designed for personal development may include goal-setting tools, habit trackers, and productivity enhancers. These tools help individuals organize their objectives and focus on personal development goals.

For individuals facing financial challenges, financial counseling services can offer guidance on budgeting, debt management, and financial planning. Addressing financial stress is a crucial aspect of holistic personal development. Financial support for educational pursuits can be found through scholarships and grants. These resources ease the financial burden of pursuing further education and skill development.

Many employers offer assistance programs encompassing various aspects of personal development, including counseling services, career development support, and wellness programs. Government programs may provide financial assistance for specific life circumstances, such as education, housing, or healthcare. Exploring available resources can alleviate external stressors, enabling individuals to focus on personal growth.

Physical well-being is integral to personal development. Fitness and wellness centers offer resources for exercise, nutrition counseling, and wellness programs that contribute to overall health. Medical professionals, including general practitioners, nutritionists, and specialists, are crucial in supporting physical health. Regular check-ups and consultations contribute to a holistic approach to personal development. Practices such as yoga, acupuncture, and massage therapy offer holistic physical and mental well-being approaches. These therapies can complement traditional healthcare approaches. Engaging in mind-body practices, such as tai chi or qigong, fosters a connection between physical and mental well-being. These practices contribute to overall balance and harmony in personal development.

As individuals navigate the intricate path of personal development, recognizing and utilizing the diverse resources available is essential. From professional support services that address mental health to educational resources that facilitate knowledge acquisition, community networks that offer social support, and technological innovations that enhance accessibility, the array of available resources forms a comprehensive support system. Financial, physical, and health resources further contribute to a holistic approach to personal development. Encouraging individuals to explore and leverage these resources empowers them to overcome challenges, deepen their understanding of themselves, and progress on their unique growth journeys. In the collective utilization of these resources, individuals foster a culture of continuous learning, resilience, and empowerment—a testament to the boundless possibilities that unfold when support is sought and embraced on the path to ongoing personal development.

Thank you for buying and reading/listening to our book. If you found this book useful/helpful please take a few minutes and leave a review on the platform where you purchased our book. Your feedback matters greatly to us.

Printed in the USA
CPSIA information can be obtained
at www.ICGtesting.com
CBHW020918120824
12967CB00038B/1225